the *Feminine* side of Leadership™

Encourage Authenticity

Create a Family

Assume Authority

Emanate Strength

Practice Kindness

Advertise Value

Inspire Creativity

Foster Growth

Cultivate Culture

Lead from the Heart

the Feminine side of Leadership™

Softening our approach for
building stronger organizations

by

Jenny Fisher

authorHOUSE®

AuthorHouse™
1663 Liberty Drive, Suite 200
Bloomington, IN 47403
www.authorhouse.com
Phone: 1-800-839-8640

This book is a work of non-fiction. Unless otherwise noted, the author and the publisher make no explicit guarantees as to the accuracy of the information contained in this book and in some cases, names of people and places have been altered to protect their privacy.

First published by AuthorHouse 5/6/2008

ISBN: 978-1-4343-5525-6 (sc)
ISBN: 978-1-4343-5698-7 (hc)

Library of Congress Control Number: 2007909921

Printed in the United States of America
Bloomington, Indiana

This book is printed on acid-free paper.

FSLeadership.com

The Leader's Prayer

Let me ...
Love them with all my heart,
Guide them with all my strength, and
Help them with all my hands,
To foster the *growth* of each individual,
and our *success* as one.

- J. Fisher

Dedication:

This book is for my mother,
who worked under the ceiling of a "man's world,"
and for my daughter,
who will never know any ceiling existed, from the cracks
and holes made by those before her.

Contents

Foreword

By Blair Christie
Senior Vice President,
Corporate Communications and Investor Relations
Cisco

The leadership principles Jenny Fisher describes in *The Feminine Side of Leadership* are predicated on the most important thing we can attain—self-confidence. Without it, leadership is not possible. With it, anything is possible. Only through self-confidence can we find the courage to be AUTHENTIC, ADVERTISE OUR VALUE and then LEAD FROM THE HEART. The self-confident leader of tomorrow will encourage and foster the sheer power of diversity for any organization—from the workplace to the community. Fisher's principles encourage you to be yourself and to seek your personal definition of excellence, while balancing the needs of others, to create a collaborative and engaging work environment.

Her principles are not gender specific. They simply have origins that are gender-based. Many of the greatest leaders I have learned from are men. Each of them has exhibited several principles outlined in Fisher's framework, including one CEO who asks for a level of work that seems humanly impossible, yet sends personal thank you notes and correspondence to all who support him. Another often comments "never let them see you sweat," but shows deep compassion and sincerity to employees, customers, and all who he engages with during times of personal need or tragedy. Conversely, I've yet to meet the perfect female leader who exhibits all of these qualities— although many do come close! The shortage of female role models further proves the need for corporations to embrace and encourage the success of women. By building both male and female role models, they will increase the performance of their entire workforce.

This book finds me at an interesting intersection during my own journey into leadership—with my family, my company, and my community—leadership of my own life. At times, I find myself in situations where I understand the logic, yet am challenged to get past the emotion. It is easy to curse being a woman during these times, but as my husband often says "that is what keeps you YOU." *The Feminine Side of Leadership* enables you to pause, remember and regroup, in order to harness your innate qualities and appreciate the unique value you bring to the table as a female and as a leader.

Introduction

$\mathcal{A}$ book on leadership is nothing new; a whole section of my bookcase is dedicated to business leadership and management advice. A book that explores our intuitive, spiritual nature is also nothing new; another section of my bookcase is filled with books that encourage us to be authentic and utilize our God-given talents to achieve greatness. What's missing is a book that explores how we can apply our inner-guidance systems—our intuitive and spiritual insights—to create a mind-shift in our current leadership practices; a book that demonstrates how we can tap into the qualities of passion, creativity, and strength to build fulfilling work environments that inspire loyalty and trust within our companies. What's missing is a book that integrates the *gifts* inherent in our humanity with the *obligations* inherent in our leadership; a book that can easily live on either side of the bookcase.

This book is not about women being better than men; instead, it examines practical ways—beneficial tactics for either gender—to incorporate feminine qualities into our traditional, more masculine, leadership approaches of "command and control." It seeks to create a blended, more balanced approach to motivating people. As most of us would agree, the predominantly masculine leadership approach of today is not a reflection of any intellectual or physical superiority, but rather a by product of the long history of men occupying our leadership positions over the past century. *It's simply what we are most used to.*

In the early 1900s, the nation's primary focus was on building the "brick and mortar" foundation of the industrial

1

and educational strength of the United States. To provide a strong focus on achieving the national objectives, the country established traditional roles with strong boundaries and limitations on its citizens based on an individual's race, gender, and social standing. In the 1950s, the country's post-war activities focused on securing the nation's financial wealth and military strength with fear-based tactics and command and control strategies—where it truly was a "man's world." In the '60s and '70s, the focus turned to independence and liberation, giving way to new concepts such as world peace, family planning, and increased opportunities for minorities and women to attend college, build careers, and reach beyond their previously accepted boundaries. People of all nationalities and backgrounds were encouraged to work hard, dream big, and create a strong foundation for the next generation. In the '80s and '90s, the information age emerged creating a "boom" in education, jobs, and ultimately, greed, resulting in fast, easy money obtained by many and lost by most as the "dot-com" bubble burst. People were encouraged to tell a good story, show exuberant financial numbers, and to "cash out" before the virtual walls crumbled. The corporate and personal corruption experienced during this era resulted in many stringent government and corporate laws, most notably Sarbanes-Oxley—regarding financial and ethical standards—stock-option limitations, and increased pressure on executive packages and buyouts. We could no longer assume ethical standards; we had to *enforce* them.

Women have always played a critical role in each of the decades; whether they were supporting the war efforts at home, fighting for equality that was slow to emerge—like Margaret Sanger, who championed birth control under the most difficult cultural opposition, setting the stage for the establishment of Planned Parenthood—or pushing their way through the corporate "glass ceiling." Throughout the various roles women have played over the past 100 years, most of their effort was concentrated on demonstrating equality and proving they were "as good as a man," with the strength and abilities to achieve similar results in education, politics, and in the corporate boardroom.

We are approaching a new era of feminine power in the twenty-first century. Women, such as my five-year-old daughter, will likely outnumber men as they are exiting college and entering our corporations in the next ten to twenty years, with few expectations or preconceived notions of any "glass ceiling." Corporations and countries are beginning to experience the strength of feminine power in action, and are encouraging this new age of leadership after tasting the benefits of improved creativity and results. The world designed by the "good old boys" is being forced to change to survive in the highly competitive, global market of today; companies are being measured and evaluated by ethical standards and operational performance, unable to comfortably chew off the fat of previous successes or social connections. In order to make it, companies need to maximize the full potential of their workforce. It's no longer *nice* to have satisfied people—it is a *requirement* for winning the corporate game.

This book explores the feminine qualities of leadership to provide a more meaningful and holistic map for the leader of today. It provides key principles that attempt to steadily build upon one another, as we progress through the mind of the balanced leader: one who incorporates both the masculine "command and control" side with the feminine "nurturing and intuitive" side. The first chapter sets the stage for great leadership by recognizing the need for us all to be comfortable with our own talents and abilities to maximize our impact to the organization. We must *"Encourage Authenticity."* Next we need to provide a strong foundation for great leadership to emerge by creating a trusting and respectful environment. We must *"Create a Family."* We must then establish a strong inner-guidance system that allows us to establish order and provide direction without compromising the individuality and creativity of others. We must *"Assume Authority."* To ensure that we provide a balance between our strong and soft leadership practices, we must be willing and able to *"Emanate Strength"* and *"Practice Kindness."* To ensure that value is consistently realized across the organization, we must set the expectations for value to be demonstrated, and use our leadership skills to increase exposure and adoption rates as we *"Advertise Value."* To maximize the potential within those whom we lead, we must consistently reinforce the positive as we *"Inspire Creativity"* while working to *"Foster Growth"* throughout the organization to encourage job satisfaction and loyalty. And finally, we must utilize our inner strength and self-confidence along with our external power as leaders to create a passionate, high-performance work environment; we must *"Cultivate Culture"* as we *"Lead from the Heart."* By the conclusion, we will have established a formula for merging conventional theories of business leadership with the more holistic theories of the new millennium to unleash the power of the individual and reach the highest potential within our organizations.

I sincerely hope that the ideas in this book help to create a new paradigm in our corporate culture and establish the importance of heartfelt leadership, leadership that seeks to value us each independently and inspire us all collectively.

Encourage Authenticity

66 Authenticity is the ability to know ourselves
and to act in ways that complement this inner-
knowledge — it allows us to actively communicate
what success looks like for ourselves and others 99

Encourage Authenticity

*M*y first corporate job—as a young, eager engineer in my twenties—was in an engineering firm full of middle-aged, sports-minded, conservative men. I hated sports, loved shopping, and had recently graduated from UC Berkeley, well known for its liberal views. I grew to loathe the lunch hour. The boys would all gather around the conference table with lunch bags and newspapers in hand, ready to debate, theorize, and pontificate about the world at hand. As a recent graduate in a male-dominated field, I assumed this was the "real world" and that I not only had to accept it, but had to zealously try to prove that I could fit in.

During the first few lunches, I nodded along, and feigned interest as they fought over football teams, or agonized over the stock market. I considered myself a bright, interesting person, but in those lunch hours, I felt as exciting as one of the brown paper bags on the table. Similarly, I felt uninspired by the drone engineering work I was assigned, composed of endless piping and instrumentation diagrams, mind-numbing computer simulations, and the drudgery of report assembly. I wasn't inspired and was growing more certain each day that there had to be more to this corporate world. I was an average engineer doing average work, in a job that had largely been father-prescribed.

Then my world changed. I discovered that I was really good at translating technical content into a visually pleasing, easy-to-understand format, which was previously lacking in our training programs, customer proposals, and marketing materials. I looked for every opportunity to help add value to our training and marketing activities. Managers took notice. They liked what I was developing and asked me to participate in these activities more and more. I quickly found myself spending most of my day on the projects I enjoyed and less and less time with my old friends, the piping diagrams.

My progression seemed to happen very quickly—as if overnight, I had become happier and more productive in the same small office that had just recently been crushing my dreams. I had created a new perception of the "real world" for myself. Once I got involved with work that I really enjoyed, I stopped joining the noon conference table. Most often, I was too busy and caught up in the work, but also found other avenues for lunch time, such as meeting friends at a local café, enjoying the bridge view, or just going for a walk around the city. I learned that it was OK to be myself, and found that I had much more to talk about with my male colleagues after finding some common ground in our interests and actually *enjoying* my discussions with them. When I did find myself at the noontime conference table, I no longer had to "fake it" and was able to be an active part of the lively interactions.

Once I figured out how to use my passion and skills to create value in the company, everything seemed to fall into place. I then realized my original mistake of trying to fit my "square peg" into the "round hole" they had defined for me. I had assumed failure as I grew more frustrated from fighting against an imperfect fit. I didn't realize that I had to *discover* my own "sweet spot," and then aggressively seek out the opportunities which showcased my skills. Finding my *authentic self* had created so much positive energy and attracted so many new growth opportunities that I was soon given promotions within my first job, which eventually led to other key opportunities in my career development—all because I hadn't continued to fight a bad fit, but had looked for ways to adapt and change the requirements. I learned—and have continued to re-learn throughout my career—the value that I can offer others and where I can best apply this value to succeed in what I do.

Authenticity is the ability to know ourselves—the things that make us happy, inspired, and fulfilled—and to act in ways which complement this inner knowledge. It is a prerequisite for personal success, and a fundamental requirement for a leader who is responsible for providing the motivation and work environment for others to succeed.

Throughout my career, I have observed that trying to "fake it" doesn't work. You can try to look or act a certain way, but unless you find a way to be yourself, things rarely go well. Although we may often find ourselves in situations or with people who are not in exact agreement with our personal beliefs or choices, we can learn to effectively deal with these "non-ideal" external situations in a way that *is* consistent with our inner, authentic self. While it is important to be confident in our own personality and beliefs, it is equally important to be accepting of those who may not have similar tastes and interests. There will always be many kinds of people and hoping or pretending that you can surround yourself with people just like yourself is simply not realistic—or very enlightened. It would be a very boring world if we were all the same! This is especially true in the corporate environment, where you generally have little to no control over choosing the people above, below, and next to you in the organization.

A balanced leader is able to be tolerant of others while maintaining her personal beliefs and individual style. Being accepting of someone's differences does NOT mean that you need to pretend to know more than you do, have connections that you don't, or suddenly want to pursue a new life dream. Being accepting DOES mean that you seek to understand another person's viewpoint and look for something in their interests or background to uncover a common ground between the two of you. In my experience, people who may appear to be very different externally often possess some of the same interests and values that can help foster communication and the basis of a good working relationship. *Finding common ground uncovers the value in our relationships and helps us to better understand and motivate others.* We cannot hope to find any value by taking the easy way out and focusing on, or complaining about, the obvious differences. Finding commonality is to the benefit of both parties, and ultimately the organization, as it increases the comfort level and leads to a win-win situation for both. Increasing the comfort level encourages co-workers to focus on the important aspects of their job rather than interpersonal quirks or gabbing about glib e-mails or comments, the things that might gnaw at us on the drive home or give way to sleepless nights.

Authenticity is one of the most important factors in becoming an effective, well-respected leader. It requires that we are fully aware of our personal strengths, weaknesses, needs, and preferences. This awareness can only develop from experiencing successes and failures, likes and dislikes, and the positives and negatives that enable us to differentiate and draw conclusions regarding our authenticity. It requires that we've seen the good, the bad, and the ugly. Authenticity requires a leader to develop a strong personal tuning system, an intuition, which instinctively draws us toward a situation, or protectively repels us from it. A leader's inner convictions must allow for tolerance, but never indifference. Rather than passively assuming results, our authenticity actively guides us to define and progress toward our personal success.

The balanced leader uses authenticity to *actively* communicate what success looks like for herself and others. She realizes that she cannot rely on external factors or relationships to guarantee her rite of passage; she must take the responsibility to clear her own path.

She applies her authenticity as she leads through the following:

- She is sensitive to emotions and external factors which impact her well-being; she knows how to open-up to increase her connection with others and how to shut-down to protect herself in dangerous territory.

- She is confident in her strengths and weaknesses; she brings a unique set of qualifications and skills to the table that enables her to be successful.

- She is prepared for the detours or roadblocks ahead; she understands that situations are rarely perfect. She relies on her "inner GPS" to keep her tracking toward her purpose, and she doesn't easily fall prey to outside influence or external definitions of success.

- She encourages authenticity in others; she inspires an authentic environment and encourages others to develop their own inner guidance as well.

Authenticity is not a new concept. Many motivational speakers and books emphasize its value when defining our overall purpose and goals in life. Leadership concepts, however, need a stronger, new connection to the value that authenticity brings to defining the culture and respect within our organizations. We see too many leaders in our corporations today who will suddenly change their tune based on the influence or perceptions of someone else—in many cases, trading their inner authenticity for external acceptance.

If we were all machines, we could easily program our business objectives, quarterly goals, and task lists each day, and we would get the requested employee output and operating earnings. If it were that easy, we would only need frontline supervisors and would not be dependent on the leadership qualities within our companies to dictate success. Fortunately, our people are the foundation of our corporations and our leaders have the ability to unlock the powerful potential that resides within them. A leader cannot fully unlock this potential if she is not confident in her own strengths and abilities or is unable to demonstrate her own authenticity to others.

Authenticity allows the leader to look outside of herself to objectively seek the truth. A demanding or myopic leader usually looks for the truth she *expects* or *wants* to see, that fits within her desired outcome or predetermined definitions. It takes much more courage to be an authentic leader and to deal with situations that are uncomfortable, conflicting, or inconsistent with what others want or expect to hear. Preset expectations from upper management or individual agendas often contribute to a leader's "blind eye" toward his or her organization. This disconnect creates a paradox: As the leader increases her demands and expectations in a situation that is clearly not working, the employee's receptivity and confidence in her leadership steadily declines.

Authentic leaders understand and tap into their own strengths to maximize and personalize their impact with their employees. They get specific when defining their own success, and use themselves as a role model to drive unique challenges and introspection from others. *Authenticity is learning to understand, accept, and make the most of yourself first.* You don't *have* to play golf if you don't like it, you don't *have* to get up at the crack of dawn if you are not a morning person, and you don't *have* to miss dinner every night with your family, or pretend to be best friends with every executive. You may have to take a personal "deep dive" to fully understand your list of "wants" if—like most of us—you have endured the business world of "shoulds," "protocols," and "senior management directives." Being authentic allows you to be confident in knowing and being who you are and picking and choosing among the many *assumed* directives. Many times, the company directives we march to are assumed behavior from the many years of repetitive activity, the "we've-always-done-it-that-way" assumption. Being in tune with our authenticity requires that we listen to our inner voice to find our true, authentic "shoulds." Having an authentic leader empowers team members to be their authentic selves. When you get a group of highly motivated people who know and understand their own talents and joys, it can lead to amazing things. When your people feel they can be themselves, they will be more open to taking risks, giving more of their time and efforts to the company mission, and remain happy and content while they are doing it. I know from my first job that my company appreciated much more value from my role after finding where I could best contribute than when I had been bored and uninspired. The impacts of having corporations filled with people doing things that do not inspire, motivate, or satisfy them can be devastating, both to the corporate culture and the bottom-line results. Great companies and great leaders realize the value of the individual and understand that the more authentic people they employ, the greater the benefits to the organization.

Authenticity does not come about suddenly, and can't be preached about conceptually. While authentic leadership may sometimes be a subtle factor in leadership tactics, it carries an enormous weight in how well the leader is respected and followed within an organization. It can't be faked in a meeting or company presentation, but is demonstrated unconsciously through the leader's words, body language, and actions that happen every day throughout each interaction in the organization.

Encourage Authenticity — Personal Exercise

Find a quiet, uninterrupted space with two pieces of paper:

On the first page, put a line down the center:

1. On the left side, write, **"Leadership Traits I Admire."** Write a list of traits that <u>you admire</u> in a leader, including all details such as personal style, work ethic, communication preferences, etc. Take parts of all the bosses, family members, community leaders, or other influential leaders that you have experienced, read about, or admired in your lifetime.

2. On the right side, write, **"My Leadership Traits."** Write down <u>your personal traits as a leader.</u> Tap into any experiences you have had leading teams in your work or personal life. Be sure to be *truthful,* including the positive and negative traits that you typically display. Try to write the list as if you are coming from an external perspective, as if someone from your team were writing the list.

3. Compare the lists. Note the similarities and the differences.

On the second page, put a line down the center:

1. On the left side, write, "**Continue.**" Write the traits that match between those traits that you admire and those that you currently utilize. These are the traits that you feel good about and should continue to build upon and look for in those who you work for and work with in your personal and work environments.

2. On the right side, title "**Improve.**" Write the traits that you currently employ that are not in alignment with those that you admire. Write good <u>action statements</u>, such as, "Empower Others," "Actively Listen," etc.

3. Keep this list in a workspace or drawer and actively refer to it.

4. Schedule yourself to repeat this exercise every six months and see how the lists change. The goal should not be to eliminate the "Improve" side of the sheet, but to look deeper into your actions and styles and maintain a focus on self-monitoring and personal improvement.

Encourage Authenticity — Team Exercise

1. Have your team members complete a personal evaluation of their own leadership and teamwork traits. There are many evaluation tools for personality measurement in the work place and many are available online.

2. Talk with your human resources department or consider conducting peer-to-peer evaluation exercise with all team members. This should be done in a controlled and confidential manner to ensure that all feedback is open and honest and does not negatively impact the responder.

3. Each person should evaluate his or her personal survey along with their peer team feedback and determine what characteristics or traits are positive and should be continued, and those that are viewed as negative and should be improved.

Create a Family

“A common bond of trust and respect can turn any team into a family — encouraging each individual to engage and contribute to the team's success **”**

Create a Family

I've been a part of many great teams in my career. While they varied in purpose, industry, and countries, the best teams have all shared a common feeling—they felt like a family. These teams provided enough independence to allow each of us to thrive and grow as individuals, but held us together with a collective "glue" that united us in our commonality— we needed each other to accomplish our goal. I've also been on a few bad teams—the kinds that seem to endlessly meander along without purpose or much concern for other members of the team—these teams usually leave everyone with a universal feeling of separateness and cynicism. While the best and worst teams may all produce an end-result, it takes a great team to provide the "glue" that makes everyone feel comfortable and necessary; this "glue" turns the team into a family.

What is the recipe for this "family" glue? Will a universal formula carry the same "stickiness" across all different types of industries and people? To answer this, we can look at our families within our homes: Do all families look alike? Do we have the same rules and ways that we spend our free time? Of course not; if you look across our various families, you'd see very different beliefs, activities, and priorities. However, what you would also see is a *common thread* that unites our family members together, a common "glue"—be it our bloodlines, personality traits, housing, vacations, or simply the sharing of our life experiences. This commonality provides us with a comfortable environment that allows us to make mistakes or try new things, surrounded by the trust and familiarity of those around us. A leader can tap into this phenomenon through the realization and reinforcement of a *common bond with the people of the team.* People have to care to effectively engage, and they have to trust in order to take the risk of *caring* for others. This common bond and trusting relationship has the potential to create a "family environment" in our often dry and distrusting corporate organizations today.

Does this "family" trait mean that all things are perfect and everyone naturally gets along with one another? As anyone can attest to from their childhood, disagreements and arguments are core aspects of any family, from sibling rivalry to which TV channel is selected, dysfunction is expected to occur. However, along with this dysfunction, we also get the very rewarding experience of feeling loved and appreciated by a group of people we trust and share our life experiences with. While we may not like everyone, we accept everyone with their unique personalities and traits. Each family member typically finds a niche role to play in the family and learns how to both differentiate him or herself while maintaining an active part of the family unit. This family unit ties everyone together in a shared commonality, yet gives everyone their personal freedom and recognition as an individual, and as a unique contributor to the group. It allows us to let our hair down, wear baggy sweats, and be comfortable as we laugh, cry, or stumble through the good and bad times together. *It provides us a comfortable environment to be ourselves.*

"Family-style" leadership is similar to a "family-style" restaurant, in which everyone dishes out their individual portions from a shared meal. Family-style dining requires that you all agree to the same meal and go about sharing it together, as opposed to just sitting with the team and ordering your own individual meal choices. Family-style leadership goes deeper than traditional teamwork; some may have to make sacrifices for the sake of the group and share their personal likes and dislikes to get what they want: "I can't stand spinach, but if we get the potatoes, I'll compromise." You learn that the team includes a potato lover, a spinach lover, a low-carb enthusiast, and of course, a junk-food junkie; *you learn about the personal needs of each individual.* You also learn that you have some team members who readily give you their requirements and some that you have to pry out with a crowbar: *you learn the best approach to engage each individual.* If you do it right, with all needs accounted for, you will maximize the outcome and satisfaction of each individual and help develop good camaraderie between team members.

So the "family-style" approach may be good in a restaurant, but why do we need it in business? Does it appeal to all personality types and preferences? How do you define it, measure it, and determine if it will have the right outcome on your team's dynamics? These are good questions for the balanced leader to ask when trying to develop her best leadership approach. As leaders, our first step is to acknowledge the successful attributes of leadership; only then will we be able to look for practical ways to build them into our team culture and appreciate their benefits. The points below show the *attributes* of the "family-style" leadership approach, followed by the *benefits* to the organization:

Traits of "Family-Style" Leadership

1. **The Team is Brought Together in a Safe Environment**.
    Most people prefer to feel like they are part of something and contribute to the overall success of a cause, initiative, or company mission. They can contribute most freely when the environment encourages recognition of both the individual and of the group. When people sense they are pulling together in a non-threatening environment, they tend to:
    *   feel more comfortable sharing experience, best practices, and past outcomes
    *   feel confident that they are contributing to the "big picture"
    *   feel the momentum and pursuit of a common goal
    *   come to understand and know each other better

2. **Everyone Feels Unique and Appreciated.**
    While recognizing the importance of the group as a whole, it is equally important to recognize and appreciate each individual contributor to the team. When people have a clear understanding of the talent, experience, and skills that each person brings to the team, they:
    - know that their contributions will be valued
    - support well-defined roles and responsibilities for each person
    - realize that each person has his or her own set of traits; some greater, some lesser, but ALL recognized and accepted
    - trust that they will each have their own "time to shine"
    - are comfortable that each person is treated fairly and individually without favoritism or special treatment

3. **Communication Is Emphasized.**
    In order to ensure the group is exposed to actions and ideas across the team, communication must be a priority. This includes:
    - regular meetings where everyone is kept current
    - open-door access to team members and leaders
    - listening and openness to thoughts and ideas
    - requiring all team members to fully engage
    - reinforcing cross-level communication in the organization—up, down, and across the team

4. **People Are Encouraged to Take Risks.**
    Team members need to feel that it is OK to make a mistake and that no one can hit the ball "out of the park" every time. As part of a healthy, secure environment, they can begin to rely more on the team results than solely on their own performance, becoming more empowered to extend themselves into new areas and develop new ideas. Being comfortable with taking risks includes:

- being empowered by the leader to try new things and stretch
- establishing a comfortable environment which is never competitive or harassing
- encouraging brainstorming to tap into the knowledge and experience of other team members
- providing initiative for driving new ideas or tasks in the group

5. **There Is a Clear Head-of-Household**.
   An effective family has clearly defined roles and expectations. In business, it is critical to have an insightful leader who sets the tone and establishes the rules for the group. When a leader is strong and effective, the team feels more comfortable and secure. An effective leader will:
   - set the rules of the game, monitor individual activity, and offer help to resolve issues and disputes
   - make decisions and act decisively in a consistent manner
   - facilitate group consensus to make sure everyone is actively engaged (not just the extroverts)
   - mediate communication and activity with other teams external to the group

6. **Emotions are Encouraged and Respectful**.
   It is important to remember that teams are groups of individuals, each bringing his or her own personality, emotions, and life situations to the table. Trying to ignore emotion and personality of team members is the fastest way to kill the creativity, teamwork, and the benefits of a family-style environment. to encourage emotions:
   - Laugh together, often and loud! There is rarely a shortage of humorous material for a group of people working hard together, especially in the corporate world.

- Let employees feel comfortable venting concerns about situations and people; it's much better to deal with emotions up front and directly, as opposed to letting them build up or endure members talking behind each other's back.
- Make sure every person is respected and comfortable showing emotions (keep Kleenex in your office if you need to be a shoulder to cry on).

Once these traits are embraced and achieved, the benefits of this leadership style will be apparent and continuously expanding. Considering the potential benefits of a leadership style can also help a leader to determine the key areas to emphasize within their own team and across the organization. While the benefits can be numerous and may vary by business, some of the more common benefits are listed below.

The basic premise of "family-style" leadership is that people operate better when they have a trusting, comfortable environment and feel connected with the people they work with.

Benefits of "Family-style" Leadership:

1. **People become more committed to their job and the company.**
   - They *work harder* and focus more on outcomes and deliverables.
   - They take *ownership* and are more accountable for their responsibilities and role in the team.
   - They *are accountable* for their personal actions and the actions of their teammates.
   - They *take less sick time* and fewer personal days, and manage days off around the needs of the team/job.

2. **They focus on the benefits of the team, not their own agenda.**
   - They *help others* to compensate for mistakes or time out of the office.
   - They *cross-train* and seek to understand and share knowledge.
   - They *increase skills and knowledge* and encourage expansion and growth of all individuals and the team.
   - They *are proactive* asking for help, making recommendations, and offering to help make everyone's job easier and the end product/service better.

3. **The team is more functional and agile.**
   - They *understand the needs outside of their own role* and they appreciate other team member's subject matter expertise and value.
   - They have *better career development and growth opportunities* in the future and look for ways to exceed in their own area and also tap into other subject areas of expertise in their group to increase their knowledge.
   - They have *increased flexibility* in accessing different thinking/execution styles, schedule coverage, planning, and tactics.

4. **They take more risks and bring the group to a higher level of performance.**
   - They *are inquisitive* and challenge others to justify recommendations, thought processes, or expected benefits.
   - They *focus on the group outcome*, to maximize benefits across the widest area.
   - They *take pride in expansion* of knowledge and progress across the individuals and the overall team. Confident and secure in their own roles, they

realize that when each individual gets better, the team gets better.

- They develop into *a continuous-improvement environment* and prefer to challenge the status quo and work toward eliminating complacency.

5. **They care about the outcome of the team/company.**
   - Members *feel accountable* for their ability to impact the company culture.
   - They feel a *responsibility to the other team members* and take their personal actions and comments more seriously.
   - They are *compelled to engage* and speak up about disagreements or recommendations on company or job vision and direction.
   - They feel a true sense of *responsibility toward employee and customer satisfaction* for their own success and that of the team.

So the benefits look good; how can we go about getting it?

"Family-style" leadership can take a while to cultivate across a group, then one day—when joking with a colleague, solving a problem, or celebrating a big win—you suddenly realize the "family feeling," the connection and dependency you have formed with your team. As a leader, I have asked myself the question:

> *"Is this connection something that just happens automatically with a group over time, or comes about naturally when people solve a challenging task together, or can we <u>actively</u> cultivate it within our teams?"*

I have determined that while it is possible for this "family" connection to occur organically over time, it can happen much quicker, with more consistency and predictability, if it's accepted, desired, and cultivated actively by the leader from the start.

How can a leader create this "family-style" environment? The following list provides some examples of how a leader can proactively enable this environment "on purpose," rather than hoping that the comfort and teamwork will happen "magically" through the typical course of the team evolution.

How to Cultivate "Family-style" Leadership

1. Define your team/family, with all roles and responsibilities clearly spelled out and shared with each team member.

2. Make sure each person has the tools needed to fully participate in their role and add value to the team. Continue to monitor and ask to ensure value and contribution to the team effort.

3. Make being part of the team important: make scheduled time for the team and expect that all respect this time equally; hold weekly team meetings; hold team events.

4. Appreciate the talent and performance of each person on the team, regardless of his or her level or reporting lines.

5. Encourage cross-departmental communication and knowledge transfer. Actively market your team's abilities and wins, and use the team to back each other up. Share capabilities from your team to another to increase exposure and opportunity.

6. Do team outings to encourage teamwork and learn more about each other's life outside of work.

7. Kill any anti-teamwork behavior immediately; let it be clear—without embarrassing or putting team members on the spot publicly—that it will not be tolerated.

8. Encourage and take in all new ideas; evaluate or give contributors the opportunity to research or validate the new idea. Create an open environment where all ideas are heard, while being practical about the time to evaluate and implement.

9. Focus on what your team delivers, rather than on other people's perceptions of you or your team. Don't trade your team's needs for senior management impressions.

10. Say only good things about your team. If faced with a performance issue, deal with it quickly and directly rather than complaining or disregarding it.

11. Be consistent in your attitude and activities so your team knows what (and when) to expect.

12. Be appreciative and say "thank you" privately and publicly in big and small ways.

13. Encourage personal growth and expansion, even if it means losing your best people—your reputation will grow for developing great people and you'll never need to worry about having "an empty nest."

14. Promote from within whenever possible and quickly assimilate external hires into the team and "family" culture.

15. Have fun and laugh often!

When a team is working well together, they propagate their satisfaction and success internally and externally, impacting employees, customers, suppliers, and competitors. They act as great ambassadors in the marketplace. When customers see the impact of improved teamwork and accountability, they will provide positive feedback, increased recognition, and new business. This, in turn, provides more goodwill to be recycled back into the team, strengthening and increasing their teamwork even more. This "goodwill domino effect" will have an amazing impact on employee satisfaction and corporate performance, with human insight and leadership skill as the only investment requirement.

Create a Family — Personal Exercise

1. Visualize your team members. Think about the unique traits or skills that each individual brings to the team.

2. For each unique trait or skill, think about how you can more fully tap into, recognize, and reward that trait to succeed in your team/organization's objectives.

3. Think of ways you can encourage each individual to share their trait/skill with other team members to increase the bonding with the team members, and also recognize the uniqueness within each team member.

4. In your next individual meeting, talk with the team member about his or her unique trait, to ensure they know the value and contribution they bring to the team. Ask them if they have any ideas for how they can further contribute.

Create a Family—Team Exercise

1. Start an activity to help increase the sharing and comfort level between your team members. For instance, in your weekly meetings, have one individual selected to share his or her background, including work experience, projects, personal activities, family, or other information they would like to share. Rotate this "employee of the week" throughout all team members.

2. Take your team out to a group dinner or activity after this exercise. Try to leverage the commonality found through some of the individual summaries.

3. Make a point of reviewing the need for having an inclusive, trusting environment with your team. Ask them if they have any ideas for how to create and sustain this environment.

4. Have regular checkpoints with your team to ensure that a safe, trusting environment is being maintained.

Assume Authority

" Authority need not be forced or proven, but
rather acknowledged and utilized to provide
the necessary governance for the team "

Assume Authority

*G*reat leadership opportunities have come about in my career from being at the right place at the right time, which has helped to reinforce my belief that "luck" is when preparation meets opportunity. In order to take advantage of these leadership opportunities, I have had to jump right in, with little to no time to justify my position, prove my worth, or do my preferred level of homework—I've simply had to *assume* my authority as a leader. The first few times I was thrust into these sudden leadership roles, I thought that my presumptuous reaction was required due to my lack of time or knowledge in a new business area; however, what I later came to understand is that this instinctive reaction became the driving force behind my ability to quickly integrate and establish respect within a new team. I discovered that assuming my role let me cut through my own internal bullshit—*the imagined perceptions created from my own insecurities*—to immediately look for ways to add value as a leader. So I assumed, and I led, and I was happy, and the team moved forward; there was no magic involved: We just focused on getting the job done together.

An effective leader must establish control and respect within the team in order to move the group in a uniform direction. She must exude a powerful energy that makes others *see value* in the end point and *have the desire* to join her in the journey. Some leaders create this energy by using their position to force their will over others, demanding authority, to initiate action. While this may result in tasks accomplished and objectives met, it rarely motivates or inspires loyalty. Conversely, some leaders fear their power and do not use authority adequately, afraid of disrespecting or upsetting their subordinates. While this may create a "comfortable" environment for the people, it rarely drives people and the organization to desired levels of performance. The balanced leader does not force or fear their use of authority; she simply *assumes* it.

A leader can save valuable time and energy by assuming her authority. It allows her to avoid the power plays, self-serving speeches, or manipulation required to *prove* her authority to others and allows her to focus on delivering real value to the team and the organization. When we look past the drama, politics, and judgments, we can provide the focus needed to lead our team. People respond to a fair and confident leader; they want to stand behind someone they trust and value. When we assume our authority properly, we confidently accept our responsibilities as a leader and define "leadership" as an *active verb*—something we have control over—as opposed to a passive title we need to vehemently defend.

The balanced leader understands that using her authority effectively strengthens her own leadership and also inspires team members to confidently assume their personal roles and value in the team. She strives to provide a good role model that encourages others to assume their own responsibilities as well. By assuming that we each have the authority and skills to execute our individual roles, we remove the element of *fear*, and replace it with the *expectation* that we will reach our goals—similar to the confidence inspired by a programmable guidance system in our car. By programming our destination, we can eliminate the chaos of maps, cell phones, or wrong turns and devote our full attention to driving safely and efficiently.

Assuming authority is easy to say, but difficult to deliver, as it requires the leader to believe whole-heartedly that she is deserving of her position and can deliver the desired results. The balanced leader must learn to leverage her *authenticity* (as covered in the previous chapter) to help provide her with the confidence needed to assume her position. Her personal confidence is a *requirement* for her to effectively motivate and inspire confidence within others. She is not cocky, offensive, or a "know-it-all" thinking that she has all the answers, but rather makes it readily apparent that she *needs* guidance and support from others and is *reliant* on her team and those around her to take the team forward. Her confidence is in her ability to lead and inspire the collective power of the team, not just in her individual contribution.

Masculine and feminine perspectives on authority are very different. As young girls and boys, we are taught at an early age that boys need to "act tough" and not show signs of weakness, whereas girls are "protected" and must seek approval and permission from others. Stereotypes prescribe that girls tend to excel in schoolwork and follow the rules, while boys tend to enjoy competition and like to prove their strength over others. Although this traditional perception has begun to shift to a more balanced expectation across both genders, *a large gap remains between how men and women view their use of and comfort with authority.* When we tap into the appropriate traits that maximize our authority, we can optimize our inner confidence and our external strength and create a balanced approach that both commands performance and inspires the loyalty and respect from our team. We can develop a more balanced organization by first creating the balance within ourselves.

The feminine side of authority requires great trust and consistency in the leader's intuition and judgment. It requires much work, as the leader must go into the heart of the organization to properly understand and intuit its needs, execute against those needs, and monitor the effects to ensure positive results. *This pattern of intuition, execution, and follow-up are critical to building consistent results and loyalty within an organization.* The balanced leader uses her authority to make things better and continues to learn things along the way to help redirect and fine-tune her approach.

She won't rely solely on consultants to dig through the details or biased reports from her managers: *she uses her authority to properly understand the truth before she jumps in to take action.*

A leader *Assumes Authority* through the following actions:

1. **She is confident—but not overbearing.** In her dealings with others, she always demonstrates confidence. She is careful to not be overbearing or act defensively with others. Her goal is to use her skills when needed, not to overpower the skills or energies of those on her team.

2. **She is not fearful of others' perceptions or judgments.** She looks for the facts and uses intuition to guide her decision-making. She chooses the best solution for those impacted, not based on the best political move or the easiest path.

3. **She adjusts her power for each situation.** She recognizes when she is needed to set the tone and drive the group. She doesn't need to exert her power at every situation, but instead looks for opportunities to empower others or to give them experience in leading a project or team. She can be comfortable down-playing her authority and letting others lead if she is not needed, and she is equally comfortable taking control quickly if she needs to regain control to establish clear objectives. She calibrates her style based on the need of the team, not on her personal agenda.

4. **She makes her expectations known.** She maintains a consistent goal and helps others to see the rationale behind her approach. She doesn't surprise or suddenly change her direction without explanation. By clearly communicating her expectations, getting buy-in from her team, and keeping goals consistent, she is able to

use her authority most effectively and build respect and loyalty.

5. **She is aware of her impact on others**. She understands the importance of the role of the leader and chooses to use her power carefully. Similar to raising children, she is aware that a sharp word or neglected response can negatively impact the relationships with her team. She works to keep a positive approach in her style with others and is sensitive when providing constructive guidance and feedback. She strives to encourage and guide, never to overpower or neglect.

It is important for a leader to have great inner strength and conviction when assuming authority at any level of leadership, whether she is leading a task, team, company, or country. It is hard for anyone to follow a meek or indecisive leader. A balanced leader learns to harness the power of her authority with the internal guidance of her heart. She constantly evaluates the situation at hand and adjusts her authority level on a case-by-case basis to inspire peak performance in others. She taps into traits some consider more masculine to establish order and accountability, but tempers them with the feminine traits of intuition and compassion to avoid a command and control leadership style. The balanced leader has no need to force power on others through external control and domination, as she is comfortable in her own authority. Insightful leaders understand the value of *assuming authority* to quickly establish short-term results and to build a foundation for longer-term trust and loyalty.

Assume Authority—Personal Exercise

1. Think of one area in your life you would like to lead (a team, a department, a company, a type of business).

2. How would you envision behaving as the leader? Get very specific in terms of what you would do, want to accomplish, and how you would treat people.

3. What is keeping you from that position? Are there any things you can do to help support that group or make progress in that area without officially being "in charge?"

4. Offer help to those in the position and ask their guidance for doing some of the items you think would benefit that area. If you offer genuine help based on your interest in an area, it will help you get closer to your interests as opposed to being challenging or disrespectful to those that may be currently in charge.

Assume Authority—Team Exercise

1. Look for ways in your group to change leadership based on different teams or activities. Give practice to team members on the up and down sides of being a leader. Some will be surprised at the difficulty involved in trying to motivate and inspire others to act.

2. If appropriate, have team members rate the effectiveness of team members in a peer-to-peer feedback survey. Have team members understand and reflect on their personal leadership style and how they feel as both a team member and a leader.

Emanate Strength

> ❝ A leader must effectively use her strength to maintain a peaceful, respectful environment — one that protects the comfort and success of her team ❞

Emanate Strength

*S*trength is a requirement for great leadership. Strength requires that the leader is confident in taking a stand to support herself, her team, and her organization to consistently "do the right thing." There have been many times when I have had to "act strong" for the benefit of the group when I haven't felt very strong internally, including layoffs, organization changes, or in personal tribulations with myself or my teammates. In these times, I have tried to combine the responsibility of being a leader with the compassion of being human, to build a constructive environment for the team. It is the times that people are feeling their weakest that require the greatest strength from our leaders.

An effective leader must have inner strength to help her overcome personal barriers so she can provide guidance and support to her team. In order for her strength to be felt by the group, the leader must *Emanate Strength* outward, through the thoughts, words, and actions she uses in directing and motivating others. While staying true to her beliefs and emotions, she can use her ability to *project strength externally* — in those moments when she may *not* be feeling her personal strongest—to maintain a consistent and secure environment for her team. The balanced leader can blend the use of her strength with her sense of compassion to help guide her in her decision-making and desired action.

Strong interpersonal skills cannot make up for a leader's lack of strength. The perception of weakness can undermine any leadership initiative, no matter how noble the cause. There is always bound to be a naysayer who will try to discount or take over an initiative that lacks strength of leadership due to his or her jealousy or skepticism with the promised outcome. To protect against this, a leader needs to be able to consistently demonstrate her strength, while maintaining her softer side, in order to not alienate others. Using both strength and compassion demonstrates the dual nature of the balanced—hard and soft—leadership approach and results in the formation of healthy *respect* within the organization. This respect will help to open up channels of communication and inclusion while setting boundaries on the misuse or abuse of power.

The balanced leader must look for opportunities to demonstrate her compassionate strength on a daily basis to ensure the protection and security of her team. If she can see a potential threat coming, then she can confront the issue early and work to settle it promptly, saving her and her team the emotional and physical trouble of fighting against an unimportant issue. Whereas an unbalanced leader—who has a primarily masculine approach—may put her energy toward preparing for and engaging in the battle she *expects* to happen. By exercising her feminine side—as the protector of peace—the leader could avoid battle altogether, and save valuable time and energy before the "troops" are engaged. She learns how to effectively maneuver her use of strength to protect and maintain a peaceful, respectful environment, and realizes the absurdity of fighting to obtain peace.

It takes much positive emotion and personal energy for a leader to constantly monitor and react to the potential threats that may attack her team. To ensure that she always has enough energy reserves, the leader needs to look for opportunities to constantly refresh her inner strength and enthusiasm. She should look to keep reminders of her past successes to help fuel her motivation and actively engage her team members to keep the energy levels high. The leader must become very in tune with the subtle signals and events that impact energy levels. Through her guidance, she will exploit the activities which provide positive, healing energy to the team, and confront and avoid those situations which deplete the health of the team. *She works to manipulate the energy and experiences felt by everyone to maximize the positive outcomes.*

Leaders can effectively *Emanate Strength* by learning to pay attention to and focus on the energy levels of her team and the impact of external forces. Many times, leaders will try to convey their strength through recounting past "battle stories" of companies saved, deals won, or customers rescued. This past-focused reminiscing is similar to the hunter showing off a collection of old animal trophies. An effective leader understands the power of demonstrating her strength on a daily basis. By choosing to live in the here and now, not in the past or hypothetical future, she knows that her actions and decisions of *today* will determine her strength and influence of *tomorrow* in the organization. Although she lives in the present, she does not disregard her past, as she realizes the great wisdom and experience that she can extract from it. A leader's strength is maximized if she takes the wisdom and lessons learned from her past successes and failures and applies them to her *present actions.* This approach helps a leader to be both humble and strong, as she realizes the fleeting nature of success and failure. She knows the greatness of her strength and power, but is reminded daily that there will always be someone brighter, faster, or more "connected to the top" than she.

Emanating strength is a leadership skill that can be learned, applied, and continuously improved. Since it is dependent on the leader's ability to harness and project her personal power, her actions must be consistent and authentic with her personal beliefs. There is no short-cut to perpetuating a leader's strength; it must be patiently cultivated on a daily basis to carry the necessary influence with others.

The balanced leader works to **Emanate Strength** through the following actions:

1. **Set the Direction.** A strong leader must be specific about what she believes in and what she wants to accomplish. This allows her to effectively guide her team in a unified direction and reinforces her strength and conviction. She realizes that if she is vague or does not take adequate time to define her expectations, she may mislead her team or be easily influenced by others. She does not let the details overwhelm or intimidate her ability to set the direction she is leading in. She knows the value of setting the direction and she readily communicates it to others.

2. **Overcome Fear.** The sensitive leader realizes that negative words and actions come from our fears—fear of failure, fear of ridicule, or fear of looking like we don't know what we are doing. Acting from fear is contrary to good leadership. Many times, a leader will take the more passive approach, hiding or avoiding the things that she is afraid of. The most effective leaders understand their fears—the situations, people, and tasks that they are not familiar with or dislike—and learn to face them head on. A leader can use her inquisitiveness to counteract her fear by approaching a fearful situation with the attitude, "How can I improve this?" or, "What can I learn from it?"

3. **Be Proactive.** An effective leader doesn't avoid confrontations; she will put the screaming voicemail, the difficult conversation, the awkward meeting at the top of her list. This eliminates the energy wasted dreading or avoiding it and increases her comfort level the next time she has to face it. When she encounters abrasive people in her career, she deals with them politely and efficiently, and seeks to better understand the source

of their behavior to help her adjust her communication style to maximize their combined outcome.

4. **Take a Stand.** The balanced leader understands the need for standing up for her decisions and choices. She doesn't continually sit on her "soap box" or spout endless advice, but instead, remains steady in her key principles, those that she considers to be non-negotiable. She will not easily "sell out" her ideas or beliefs based on their popularity, and is not afraid of carrying a unique or different viewpoint in a group. She has a strong sense of her inner beliefs and strives to speak her mind in a respectful, constructive manner.

5. **Manage Conflict.** Leaders need to accept that everyone is unique and has differing opinions and experience. The balanced leader sees value in these differences and encourages others to display their *real* insights and ideas. The leader needs to be comfortable in her own skin, and encourage others to share their thoughts and concerns in a non-threatening environment. She must *value* conflict, and actively manage through it to make sure it results in a positive, best-case outcome. She doesn't challenge or intimidate others with her opinions, but instead, presents her thoughts and encourages feedback.

6. **Push Back.** Much like managing conflict, it is important for the leader to be strong when someone is challenging her beliefs or behaving in a way she feels is counterproductive to the mission of her team. If she is challenged, she sees it as an opportunity to better understand their concern, and does not immediately discount their opinions or label them "wrong." The balanced leader has learned the *art* of combining the strength of her convictions with the sensitivity of her intuition and communication style to counter opposing

ideas appropriately. She seeks to listen effectively in order to understand the other person's viewpoint, and then offer ideas to expand their collective thought process *together*.

7. **Choose Your Battles.** The balanced leader understands that every issue cannot be urgent, and every conflict cannot be won. She uses her intuition to appropriately judge a situation and assess its level of impact. If it is something that will likely carry a large, negative impact to her and her team, she will properly defend and protect. If it is something that will likely carry little or no impact, she will not resist it. She saves her team's energy for the issues that count and is careful to not let her "ego" (or others' perceptions) determine her battle decisions.

The balanced leader is aware of the personal power she carries, and knows how to use it with external people and situations to maximize a positive outcome. She *Emanates Strength* to protect and defend the peaceful environment within her team and to maximize their ultimate contribution to the organization.

Emanate Strength—Personal Exercise

1. Think about a group situation in your past that caused you to feel weak or inadequate. What did it feel like?

2. Think about how you could have better prepared for the situation. Could you have been less reactive or more open to another's opinions?

3. Imagine how the situation would have played out if you had felt really strong. Replay the event with a feeling of strength, envisioning you had adjusted your actions as needed.

4. Make a reminder list of the things you will do differently in this situation to develop your inner strength and to emanate this strength onto others.

Emanate Strength—Team Exercise

1. In your next group meeting, attack a problem that you know requires strength and conflict in your team.

2. What attributes can you bring out in your team members to encourage their truthful engagement?

3. Ask the team to bring forth any skills that would help them to explore the concept of "healthy conflict."

Practice Kindness

> **"**Kindness encourages us to treat others as we want to be treated — to be valued for our input and actively included in the outcome**"**

Practice Kindness

*U*nfortunately, when I tried to think of a good example for this chapter, one that demonstrated a great act of kindness, what came to mind first were the times when I could have been more kind, the times when I asked abruptly, scolded prematurely, or assumed wrongly. While most of us realize the need to be kind, we can also identify with the difficulty of consistently being kind when faced with the daily pressures of our own lives: personal difficulties or oversights, sudden requests from senior management, or the regular occurrence of emergencies in our fast-paced corporate environments. In order for a leader to create the environment and the individual engagement required for great performance, it is essential that we strive to *Practice Kindness* in our daily interactions as leaders. Kindness allows us to appreciate the human side of the people we work with; it helps us to develop a culture that is mutually respectful and appreciative of individual contribution. It is essential for the leader to keep "kindness" in her leadership bag of tricks, to help bring balance to the need for her to also exercise her authority and strength to effectively direct others. Kindness helps us in our application of our needed leadership duties; it recognizes that the process of *how* we engage and interact with the people is as important— or arguably more important—than the end result that we are always hurrying to deliver.

It takes a great leader to be kind, one who is comfortable with herself and confident in her own abilities and the abilities of her team, one who has taken the time to create and visualize the big picture while considering the details and complexities inherent in its design. It is much easier to be kind if you have a path to follow and can allow for flexibility and change along the way. It is much harder to be kind if a leader has procrastinated, left things unaddressed, or left people out of the loop or tasks partially undone. This lack of preparation leads to increased frustration and fear in the leader which typically leads to negative impacts to her team, including belittlement, blame, overreaction, or guilt. Our tasks, projects, and work environments rarely go as originally intended, so it is up to the leader to prepare for the needed flexibility she will undoubtedly need as she guides her team through the process. Once this flexibility is planned for, it will give her the needed time and space to allow her to be kind.

How we treat others is a direct correlation with how we treat ourselves. If a leader gives herself the time to visualize, create, and make modifications, she will place value on the evolutionary approach and encourage others to do the same. This evolutionary approach doesn't assume that everything will be "right" the first time, or that people will execute all tasks "flawlessly." It assumes that there will be mistakes, adjustments will need to be done, and that progress will be made. If she treats herself with dignity and respect and holds herself accountable for her actions and responsibilities, she will teach her team to be accountable and responsible as well. A leader should never underestimate the power she has to impact the lives and well-being of those she leads. Once a leader realizes the potential impact she has on others, she can learn to monitor and control her emotional reactions to ensure that all interactions are positive and professional.

Some of the attributes to *Practice Kindness* include:

- *Being sensitive* to the individual needs and personality of each person they interact with.
- *Keeping positive* in her outlook, words, and actions to maintain forward motion and progress.

- *Taking a "lessons-learned" approach* when looking back, rather than trying to blame or criticize actions or people.
- *Leaving appropriate time* to react to and complete a needed activity, to refrain from creating a high-pressure environment.
- *Appealing to the help needed* and business rationale in urgent situations rather than forcing or demanding action.
- *Thanking and appreciating* all activity that is done by the team to accomplish both the everyday and urgent activities.

Kindness is an area that extends throughout all aspects of our lives, including how we interact with our families, our co-workers, and the guy behind the deli counter at lunch. If we strive to be kind throughout our interactions with everyone, we will be amazed at how much easier it is to get along with people. If we all go back to the "golden rule" in our workplaces, to treat people as we'd like to be treated ourselves—*to be valued, communicated with, and actively engaged*—we would see the loyalty and respect within our organizations increase dramatically.

There are countless situations and opportunities to convey kindness in our corporate environments. Many of us are guilty of operating on autopilot when it comes to expressing our kindness and often use external situations as excuses for our poor actions; holding how we were parented, our daily pressures, or our corporate culture to blame. We could all benefit from taking a hard look at our interactions with the various situations and people we come across daily to better understand how we can create a "kind" environment, one that is both respectful and inspiring for others. A leader must be *accountable* for her own actions, independent of the external factors that she has no control over. Once we stand up and make ourselves accountable, only then can we impart change in our behavior.

A leader can apply kindness within an organization in the following ways:

1. **Respect the Individual**: A leader needs to be respectful of the personal needs and individual styles of the individual. A leader should ensure that each team member feels she is a valued contributor to the overall team effort. A leader can effectively demonstrate this value by understanding the individual "sweet spot" and providing work and timelines that best fit with the individual's strength. The leader should always show consideration for the areas which may be sensitive or important to the individual, such as needing to leave at a certain time or other personal constraints.

2. **Use Kind Words:** A leader's word choices should always reflect calm, positive, and controlled expression. While there will always be times when requests need to be made urgently, these urgent requests should also be asked in a respectful, constructive manner, without giving into forced demands or ultimatums. If a leader has built the trust within her team, she should be able to appeal to the urgent need placed on her and engage the help of her team through their respect and willingness to support her. By asking nicely, she is empowering her team members to do the right thing to support the needs of the business.

3. **Communicate Frequently**: A leader should always strive to provide frequent, detailed communication regarding the external factors and personal requirements for her team members. If she maintains a steady stream of communication with her team, she will be more likely to keep her team on track and reduce the amount of

surprises or sudden changes to their job responsibilities. The more a leader can communicate, the better the chances are for a collective team approach to reaching the goal.

4. **Communicate Effectively:** Kindness is best expressed in the *how* of our communications rather than the content of *what* we are communicating. To do this, the leader needs to be aware of the personalities, skill levels, and growth expectations of those she interacts with. Different people respond to different styles and requests. For some, a direct, clear request is appreciated; for others, explaining the business context or rationale is needed, while some may appreciate an emotional appeal. A leader's job is to figure out the best approach for the individual and to balance that approach with the desired business need to get the job done.

5. **Have Realistic Expectations:** A leader should be careful to not make unrealistic deadlines or deliverables that put her and her team at risk. She should strive to create realistic schedules based on the current workloads and skill levels of her team and push back on upper management if unrealistic demands are made. The more accurately she can manage requests, the more accountability and respect she will create within her team and across the organization. If she is faced with a tough deliverable, she should determine the best way to "share the wealth" across herself and her team to avoid any one person feeling overwhelmed or unable to accomplish the task.

6. **Remain Calm:** It is all too easy to assume or to overreact to a sudden request or emergency. A leader needs to set the appropriate pace to ensure that the fastest, most effective results are achieved. Too often, emergencies result in hurried activity, redundant tasks, or mistakes

made from a high-pressure situation. If a leader calmly assembles her team, identifies the right approach, and makes appropriate assignments, she can keep the focus and output high while maintaining a calm and productive work environment.

7. **Reward Contribution:** A leader should always try to maximize the personal contribution and recognition for the efforts accomplished. This is especially important for efforts which go above and beyond the daily requests. A leader who effectively rewards contribution on a continual basis will create a team that is willing to do what is necessary to complete the request because they know that their work will be valued and appreciated by both the leader and the team.

A balanced leader can effectively handle the *demands* of her organization with the *kindness* of her approach. By keeping a calm disposition, creating a realistic plan, and appealing to the individual styles of her team members, she will be able to respond quickly, with kindness and respect, to maximize the results obtained by the team. Through the consistency in her approach, she will create strong relationships and loyalty with her team and increase the speed and efficiency for handling business needs. This efficiency will continue to grow until she has created a natural rhythm for handling the day-to-day job requirements as well as the unplanned emergencies that occur in a kind, professional manner.

Practice Kindness—Personal Exercise

1. Think about a time when you were not as kind as you should have been when asking or talking with a co-worker, how do you think it made the other person feel?

2. What can you do to ensure that you will react better the next time you encounter a situation?

3. What are the factors in your personal or corporate life that cause you to react abruptly or without kindness toward others?

4. How can you proactively prepare for these situations to reduce your adverse reaction?

Practice Kindness—Team Exercise

1. In your next team meeting or project initiation, ask your team members to develop Behavior Guidelines to ensure that everyone is treated with respect (such as Listen Effectively, Do Not Interrupt, Ask Questions, Ask for Help, Thank Team Members, etc.). After this brainstorming is complete, post the list in your meeting rooms or office space to encourage this behavior.

2. Ask your team members if they are receiving frequent, effective communication. What ideas do they have for improving the communication?

3. Explore ideas for recognizing employees who go above and beyond to help their teammates or to accomplish a sudden business need. Make a place in your team meetings, town halls, or newsletters to reward contributions from these team members.

Advertise Value

“An effective leader must create the *expectation* for value to be demonstrated, the *exposure* for value to be recognized, and the *adoption* for value to be realized **”**

Advertise Value

I've grown frustrated by some of the leaders prevalent in our corporate culture who consistently focus on the rhetoric they spout or the impressions they leave, with little or no attention paid to the *value* they produce. I'm tired of hearing terms such as "micro-manager" or "detail-oriented" as being negative descriptors from people to justify their superiority or lack of knowledge in their area of responsibility. Within our competitive, frenzied, management-heavy corporations, we have grown a culture that rewards "high-level," "hands-off" management styles; a culture that promotes the belief that the further you are from the details, the higher you appear in the corporate hierarchy and the less risk you have for being exposed to anything that might go wrong. *Tactical* has become a bad word, signaling that real work is required, while everyone aspires to be "strategic" and "visionary." I've seen many leaders easily justify this "high-level" approach for a variety of reasons: senior management requests, busy schedules, client meetings, etc.; the possibilities of the "I'm too important for this" reasons are endless. Our corporations have become very burdened with distractions and change, making it easy to overlook the basic needs within the organization, and even harder to consistently focus on fulfilling them. The danger of this "high-level" leadership style is that it easily propagates down the ranks, resulting in a "hands-off" organization, with little accountability felt by anyone. I've seen too many teams, departments, and organizations go down like a sinking ship, as soon as something happens that exposes the ugly details that usually lurk behind the "high-level" picture.

Many corporations accept or dismiss a leader's laziness, disinterest, or lack of knowledge under the pretense of it being their "personal leadership style" or because they are "new to the company" or "new to a leadership role." Too often, corporations plunk newcomers from the outside or promote high performers from within into leadership positions and give them no guidance on how to effectively lead within the unique environment of the organization. All organizations are not created equal, and all leaders come from a variety of individual backgrounds and differing levels of leadership experience. By *assuming* or *hoping* the leader will know what to do in the organization, the organization is greatly increasing its risk for failure. While individual leaders may produce needed results, it is very unlikely that *all* leaders will produce *consistent* results across the organization to impact overall performance expectations. By consistently applying a leadership approach that advertises the need for each individual and team to contribute value to the organization, the culture can shift to one of accountability and focused performance.

> By **Advertising Value,** *the leader will simultaneously provide the* **expectation** *for everyone in the organization to demonstrate value, while increasing* **exposure** *and* **adoption** *rates across the organization to maximize the total impact.*

A balanced leader understands the need for combining the high-level strategy of the organization with the practical details of individual and team performance. Good leaders never *assume* progress in a situation; they *challenge and prove* progress and its impact to the organization. Driving value is hard; it requires us to dig into the situation, look for issues, and apply our business judgment to accurately assess a situation and make informed decisions. It is essential for a leader to *ensure* that her organization is delivering value: internally to its employees, externally to its customers, and ultimately to its shareholders.

Too many leaders say they are "big-picture" thinkers or just want the high-level summary of a situation. As a result, we have been trained to create the "five-minute overview" that consists of what we know they want to hear, and then we move on to solve the problem ourselves. As a result, the leadership myth is revealed: A leader can't provide value to the organization if she doesn't know the *details* behind its problems. Problems are messy. They are often a collection of complex issues created from multiple variables, including customers, employees, money, time, deliverables, and bad assumptions, to name a few. There is rarely a "high-level problem" and even rarer a "high-level solution." If a leader attempts to give a high-level solution, it usually comes with a "you know what to do" expression that is received with a "nobody cares" message by the person or team in need. The balanced leader needs to be a master at getting to the root cause, *the heart of the matter,* to determine where and how much help is *really* needed.

A leader's focus should always be on imparting value to the organization—value from her *own* actions and value from the *team's* actions. To add value, you must develop and impart an intelligent and relevant perspective. You can only have an accurate perspective if you know the details behind the situation. The balanced leader knows and understands the details within her organization; she does not assume that "other people are handling it" or that people will know what to do instinctively. Instead, she takes the accountability to ensure that the organization is progressing, and anticipates trouble spots so she can provide help or greater clarity. She never assumes that she is so safe in her position, overconfident from past experiences, or connected at the "top," to blindly delegate to those beneath her. A good leader values the details because they help her to use her inner guidance and intuition to make a more complete and accurate assessment of a given situation and best communicate or interpret a 5,000-foot view. When a leader seeks to understand the details of a particular problem or situation, it gives her the confidence to step back and assess the big picture more accurately.

Details empower leaders to demonstrate real value. I've found the practices below as effective means for gathering and assessing the details to make informed actions as a leader.

Methods for Value-Added Leadership

1. **Cut to the Chase:** A leader must get to the point when trying to communicate a particular situation. You need to grab your audience, paint the picture, and give them enough of the details to make them eager to contribute to the solution. A leader needs to learn to probe, find the root of the issue, and determine what is slowing down the individual or team. Once the leader determines the underlying issue, then she can spend time gathering ideas and move quickly toward a solution.

2. **Be Inquisitive:** Ask questions. What has been done to date? What have the customer or employee reactions been? What recommendations have been considered or are now on the table? This will not only update you on the topic, but also helps the individual or team members to summarize, reconsider, and draw some natural conclusions and options.

3. **Seek Written Documentation:** Save time by reviewing documentation concerning the project or issue before you hold group discussions or meetings. It helps if you are up to speed on the topic, and reduces the frustration of those close to the issue.

4. **Find the Weak Spots and Dig!:** A leader should be scanning the information, looking for inconsistencies, exceptions, past experiences, uninvolved parties, missing elements, etc. and then focus on suspicious

areas. This can help the leader ask new or tough questions that may have not yet been considered.

5. **Do Your Homework:** Doing your homework and understanding the details allows you to draw on your experience and knowledge. If you don't have experience in a particular area, call on other colleagues or subject-matter experts to assist in the situation. Never let your ego trump your responsibility to add value. Your title is not a "magic wand" that can be taken for granted in providing you special "solution" powers.

Things to avoid when gathering the details:

1. **Don't Wait for a Blow-up:** A good leader should keep a consistent level of detail in the oversight of her team. Waiting for a big problem or urgent requests from senior management will create frustration and demonstrate your lack of knowledge about your team's activities. While there will always be issues and special requests, a leader can lessen the impact and head off much of the disruption to her team by being proactive and consistent in her approach.

2. **Don't Place Blame:** The focus should always be in gathering and understanding the details, not pointing fingers. People will be much more open to your questions and help you get what you need if approached in a supportive environment. If a problem has occurred, acknowledge that everyone makes mistakes and look for the root cause, not the individual. Handling employee mistakes in a mature, root-cause-oriented way allows an employee to save face, so he or she can learn from the situation and not repeat it in the future. Blame makes people feel defensive and less eager to make improvements or changes to their approach.

3. **Don't Make Unrealistic Demands:** Often leaders will punish the team for the leader's previous lack of attention by demanding that all work stop, or by asking for additional documentation or summaries that waste the team's time and energy. This can lead to defensive behavior from team members, and incomplete or inaccurate data. Be sensitive to the work done previously and focus on what you can do for the team, not what they can do for you.

4. **Don't Overreact:** The best method for detail-oriented leadership is to have a consistent approach for gathering information. A leader will get far more cooperation if she calmly, methodically, and quickly seeks the details needed in a relaxed, efficient manner. Energy expended on negative feedback is wasted time and energy for you and your team, and always makes the situation worse.

5. **Don't Pretend to Know it All:** Know when to dig in, focus attention, and what your boundaries are within your knowledge and background. Ask for help and be comfortable saying "I don't know." A leader needs to wear many different hats, and sometimes team members just need an objective listener or a partner to help work through a situation with them. You don't know it all and never will, and the faster a leader acknowledges this, the sooner she can provide effective guidance.

For value to be obtained from any initiative, it must be practical and fit with the needs of the organization. Practicality is an important aspect to effective leadership. We have all seen the artful, complex, and intricate white-boarded plans that never get adopted or implemented, along with the initiatives that are discussed at great length but never come to fruition. Being a practical leader ensures that you are focusing and implementing initiatives that will bring value to the organization. To be effective, a leader must also effectively

Advertise the Value Potential, to increase exposure and adoption across the organization. Too much valuable work is gone wasted in many corporations due to the lack of internal or external advertisement of the potential value to be realized.

To ensure your personal, department, or organization's value, consider these three critical variables:

1. The *Volume* of the Initiatives Completed
2. The *Quality* of the Initiatives Completed
3. The *Adoption* of the Initiatives Completed

VALUE = VOLUME x QUALITY x ADOPTION

The *Volume* of Completed Initiatives

There are always one or two individuals in an organization who boast about a great accomplishment; this can include the largest sale, biggest event, or a record-breaking project. An effective leader doesn't need to rely on one or two great wins to impress each new audience. She knows that everyone experiences a continuous stream of trials and errors alongside their imperfect record of successes and failures. This is why the volume of initiatives completed is such a key variable. The word "completed" is important to this definition, as it contributes most to the *perception* of a leader's effectiveness. While half-finished or conceptual initiatives occur regularly in the brainstorming process, especially as a company is finding its direction, they can potentially harm the perception of a leader's effectiveness in creating tangible value to the organization. Because a leader's job is to motivate and direct *others,* it is very easy for perception to quickly become reality.

Paying attention to the volume of completed initiatives is a good insurance policy to ensure that a positive contribution will be felt by the organization. You can safely assume in all areas of life and business that you will not be 100 percent successful in everything that you set out to do. This assumes a "success factor" will be applied to your work and prepares you for the various ups and downs you will experience as a leader. This further provides you with the ability to evaluate the best sources of your success and allows you to focus on those activities and initiatives that have the greatest chance of success. It allows you to maximize your personal and corporate *"success factor."*

We have all experienced times we would describe as "being in the zone," when we seem to be able to maximize our output in an effortless way. The key to consistently delivering good quality and quantity of work is looking for ways to tap into our ability for "effortless creation." When we reside in this "effortless zone," we are truly creating and working within our natural-born talents, and we are performing at our peak level. Our level of effort is largely influenced by our own perceptions while completing the task. If we enjoy a task, we may expend more time and effort, but report that the task took less effort than a simpler task we don't enjoy doing. Anyone who loves her job or has an exciting hobby knows that time seems to fly by when doing something that takes our full attention and interest.

It is not always clear if we are operating in our "effortless zone." A good indicator is to measure our ability to produce more work in less time, to analyze our efficiency. The key to unlocking our personal efficiency is found in two key concepts: **minimize the level of effort** and **understand the expectations**. Focusing on these critical concepts will allow you to assess and increase your "personal efficiency."

- **Minimize the level of effort:** When we are working on several tasks at once, time constraints force us to keep from embellishing our work with details, which do not add value to the task. Too much scrutiny or second-guessing does not add to your overall efficiency. It is extremely important that the task is done well, but it is just as important that the appropriate amount of time is spent on the task after it has met the initial requirement. An important element to minimizing the level of effort is to maintain focus within the completion of that task. Effective "multi-taskers" are able to maintain focus on more than one item at hand, and change focus as they change their tasks.

- **Understand the expectations:** It is critical to the efficiency of completing a task that the requirements are sufficiently understood before the work is started. The easiest way to decrease your efficiency is to waste time going in the wrong direction. Planning and defining the requirements are critical to any task, project, or initiative, regardless of size. Know the target audience who will be getting the results, and spend time up front to determine and document their expectations. Purposeful dialogue and getting buy-in throughout the development and execution of a task encourages adoption.

To be practical and efficient, you need to be aware of the expectations of all constituencies in order for the final outcome to be considered a success.

The *Quality* of the Completed Initiatives:

The volume of how much you accomplish is only important if you are delivering *quality* results. The quality of your output is an important factor that helps to calibrate and counterbalance your efficiency. There is little value to producing a high volume of work that does not address the needs of your end users or cannot be implemented and adopted in the organization. An effective leader can use the Quality metrics to help evaluate if she is using her time and energies wisely. Quality can be a difficult measurement, because subjective perceptions can cloud the assessment of the work completed. The best way to get an objective measurement of the quality of the work completed includes:

- **Clearly define your audience** or the recipient of the completed work. This may be your boss, a department, or a client. Proactively seek their guidance and encourage their involvement in setting expectations for the end result.

- **Determine the expected impact** by defining key variables, taking baseline measurements, or setting targets as needed prior to project completion.

- **Have checkpoints along the way.** Don't wait until the end of an extended work effort to gauge whether you are hitting the mark. Have scheduled checkpoints regularly to determine if the work you have completed to date meets the benchmarks of quality agreed to in the requirements.

- **Measure satisfaction** after the work is implemented. Similar to the initial requirements session, this session will close the loop and confirm satisfaction with the end result. It is critical to understanding recipient perceptions, as they will determine how well the deliverable will be adopted.

Whether this all happens in a few hours for a small task, or over many months for a larger project, setting proper expectations and demonstrating that a quality product was delivered is always crucial to the success of any initiative. When evaluating the quality of a project, perception is reality, and neither presentations to upper management nor "spins" put on the results, will change the ultimate value of the work produced if the end users are not satisfied.

The *Adoption* of the Completed Initiatives:

If you are efficiently producing a good volume of high-quality work, the next level is to evaluate how well the work is being adopted by the organization. Too often, leaders produce beautiful presentations and elaborate implementation plans that never make it beyond the file cabinet or the executive office. Adoption is a critical measurement, which helps a leader to calibrate her overall contribution and leadership effectiveness. Leaders must avoid the trap of "self-assumed glory" by thinking that an impressive list of completed tasks proudly shown to a boss, with little actual impact to the organization, "proves" their personal success.

The balanced leader can use the following skills to increase the adoption of her initiatives:

1. Get People Involved. While one of the biggest efficiency-busters in an organization is to do everything through task forces or steering committees, getting the appropriate level of participation from the recipients of a project is key. A formal committee is not required to elicit feedback. You can call a one-time meeting to discuss business problems/needs and lessons learned or meet with a group or individuals throughout the project. Too many times, we rush to formalize a "steering committee" and force an issue or topic to be over-analyzed or rehashed to the point of exhaustion.

A useful rule: a *task force should be created only if:*
- participants feel it is a valuable use of their time throughout the duration
- expectations and results of the group are clearly defined and measured
- there is strong leadership and support of the initiative across the organization

Pay attention to the involvement and participation of the task force. If you sense is it losing momentum, immediately recommend changes to the agenda, team, or timeframe. Your job as a leader is to make sure their time is not wasted and that measurable results are gained from the experience. A negative or disengaged task force can be worse for the adoption of the initiative than having none at all.

2. Ask for Feedback. People like to be included and consulted. Each person you ask for help or feedback is a potential champion of your initiative. Ask about their needs, problems, and ideas concerning the initiative. Ask them how this can make it better based on their past experiences, failed attempts, or previous initiatives. Nothing reduces the perceptions of a leader's effectiveness more than attempting the same approach done over and over but expecting different results. While you may not use every bit of feedback, you will gain a wealth of knowledge and experience across the organization, and probably come across a few unexpected champions who are passionate about your project. As you ask for feedback, keep the momentum high throughout the process, not just at the initial stages.

3. Advertise. One of the best ways to increase adoption for a new task or initiative is to generate some excitement and eagerness for the results. Try to advertise the goals and benefits to everyone who is involved, including the management and executive staff. Treat your internal initiatives just like you would an external product launch; complete with logos, taglines, and marketing efforts. This is a great opportunity for the leader to bring creativity into her work and to generate some fun in getting the task completed. Adding a tagline and logo to the project or group helps unite the group and brand the results of the effort. Once peripheral teams start seeing the "branded initiative," they become familiar with the concepts and are not caught off guard or surprised by the results. Advertising does not need to be limited to large-scale projects or initiatives. Managers can "socialize" their projects by introducing it at lunch or bringing it into their daily conversations and meetings across the organization.

4. Limit Surprises. If you make a conscious effort to get people involved and ask for feedback throughout the process, nothing should come as a big surprise at the time you launch your project. No one likes surprises, and they tend to feel blindsided if they feel they should have been included sooner. This can cause potential champions to reduce their support of your initiative, even if they inwardly see value in the concept or results. Keep communication levels high and limit surprises to all impacted people. Increased communication will likely increase implementation times and lessen detours from disconnected or defiant individuals who were kept out of the process.

The balanced leader instinctively looks for ways to *demonstrate* value and effectively *advertise* the value potential across the organization to achieve peak results. She strives to foster a continuous improvement culture and does not sit back comfortably or assume that her value is readily apparent to others. By learning to optimize the volume of output, ensuring quality deliverables, and building strong support and adoption from end users, she can achieve tangible results that are genuinely appreciated and used across the organization.

Advertise Value-Personal Exercise

Visualize a team member coming to you with a problem. Think back to a problem brought to you or create a hypothetical problem (the project is late due to missed deliverable, customer issue, missed sale, budget issue, personal problem, etc.):

1. Envision the employee describing the problem.
2. Focus on really listening fully to the problem.
3. Ask questions and probe to fully understand and seek out more information regarding the issue.
4. Summarize your understanding of the issue and get the team member's additional concurrence to the summary.
5. Seek *clarity* in the problem statement; write it down.
6. Examine the impact, what will happen if the problem continues? Provide perspective; is it that big in the first place? Has it happened before? Does it require immediate action or will it go away or diminish on its own?
7. Ask what solutions have been considered already. Write them down next to your problem statement.
8. Brainstorm potential solutions with the team member that may come up as a result of a new perspective. Write them along with the other solutions provided earlier.
9. Discuss the potential solutions with their required action and impact.
10. Choose the best solution together and justify why.
11. Ask the team member if she understands and can summarize the problem and decision to the team in a follow-up written communication.
12. Verify if she thinks the time spent was helpful in her thinking process, and thank her for including you in the problem-solving process.

Advertise Value-Team Exercise

1. Complete the Personal Exercise multiple times until you are comfortable with listening, probing, summarizing, brainstorming, and verifying a solution with a team member. You should feel comfortable "seeking clarity" in both the problem and solution.

2. At your next team meeting, when a problem presents itself, ask the group to spend fifteen to twenty minutes in the "Think Tank" and facilitate the above steps with the group.

3. Adapt this exercise into your regular team experiences to show the benefits of "seeking clarity" before you prioritize and set out to provide a solution.

Inspire Creativity

" Creativity is the force that transforms
our ideas into tangible outcomes —
it encourages us to be passionate and
inspired in all that we do **"**

Inspire Creativity

*G*rowing up, I would never have described myself as "creative." I was always pushed toward practical subjects like math and science so I could get a practical job that provided a decent salary and a solid career. My early perception of "creativity" involved images of rebellious, hippie-like people reading poetry in cafes or selling their canvases on the street as they struggled to make ends meet. I assumed that creativity was reserved for a select few who had dedicated their lives to create their masterpiece novel, painting, or screenplay. If you wanted a good job and a promising career, you had to be practical and work hard. Looking back now, I am amazed at how wrong I was, and how much I have used and benefited from creativity throughout my "practical" career. I have drawn upon my creative nature to create incentives for my teams to succeed, to design courses and meetings to inspire, and to build programs and materials to teach and excite. I have learned that *creativity is the force behind manifesting our thoughts or concepts into tangible outcomes.*

An effective leader must recognize and *Inspire Creativity* in order to maximize the contributions and impact made by the people in the organization. With our efficiency-driven, fast-paced environment, it is all too easy to get stuck in the mantra of not "reinventing the wheel" to ensure we are developing our end products as quickly as possible. The danger is that the "wheel" may desperately need reinventing due to the ever-present changes in our internal and external requirements and circumstances. Creativity is a natural counterbalance to our need and desire for efficiency (as we discussed in the previous chapter, *Advertise Value*). This balance between creative expression and efficient output is another example of the need for taking a balanced approach to leadership. If we relied solely on efficiency, we would be lacking in new ideas and directions; whereas if we relied solely on our creativity, we would be lacking in our performance and speed-to-market. Balanced leadership needs both: the driving, masculine side, which demands efficiency, and the creative, feminine side, which encourages us to approach things with a fresh, new outlook.

We all have the ability to turn our thoughts into reality through the creative process. Our creativity is the driving force behind our growth and progress as individuals, as teams, and as corporations. As leaders, we should welcome creativity into the workplace, give it the broadest definition possible and allow for it to be applied to everything that we touch. Creativity is part mind and part heart. It requires us to tap into our intuition and our inner thoughts to fully perceive a vision, and to then actively engage in its creation. The visual picture is required before the physical action can take place, and acts like a road map to guide us through the creation process as we are turning the non-physical into the physical. Creativity can be appreciated at all levels, from the Van Gogh masterpiece to the handmade greeting card from our children, and is just as relevant to our jobs. It allows us to put our "fingerprint" on the work that we each produce, and provides us with the single best personal differentiator in our careers. It drives our imaginations to develop new products, services, or ways to approach our day-to-day business, and leaves us with tremendous pride and satisfaction as we transform our ideas into things.

Manifesting our thoughts into things requires great confidence in our abilities and a positive, trusting environment. To inspire creativity in the organization, a leader can look to both using creativity herself and inspiring the creative process in others. To realize her own creative potential, the leader must apply two important concepts: She must *listen and trust her inner voice for inspiration,* and she must fully *recognize and draw from her personal talents.* This will enable her to effectively personalize her efforts and maximize her impact to the organization through her unique "stamp." Her confidence in her talents and trust in her inner guidance enables her to be excited about new opportunities and secure in her ability to mold a successful outcome from the images in her mind. To be creative, she must first trust—in the opportunity, in herself, and in the outcome. The creator then has to "see it" with all of the various parts coming together like instruments in an orchestra to bring it into being.

The balanced leader sees value in inspiring creativity in others. By recognizing creativity, we are able to appreciate and place value on the unique contributions from each individual in the organization. If we were all the same, like interchangeable widgets, then any of us could produce the desired results. But if our unique qualities are valued, then we should look for the best ways to apply our individual talents to the organization to maximize our personal satisfaction and organizational impact. Creativity is essential for building a continuous-improvement, employee-empowered culture. The voice of creativity says, "Show me something unique, a better way to do it, something no one has ever thought of or done before." It values a different perspective and gives a stage for everyone to play on. Creativity keeps us from doing things one way because "we have always done it this way" or because senior management said so. As many companies have shown (Apple, 3M, Google, and Crayola) creativity impacts the bottom line in employee retention, product innovation, and customer satisfaction.

Creativity allows each of us to look at a document as a canvas, a meeting room as a stage, or a lunch as a networking opportunity. It demands that we go through a "creative process" as we imagine, draft, cut, edit, and assess our work like an artist. The canvas may change, but the creative process stays the same. Once we learn to appreciate the creative process and the passion it unleashes, we look for ways to express our creativity in everything we do. A boring task can become interesting when we put our creative spin on the outcome and unlock the potential of the finished product.

The workplace is full of Van Gogh paintings, Mozart compositions, and Shakespearean plays being created every day. For the leader to inspire creativity, she needs to actively seek these creative opportunities for her team members and recognize the benefits of creative contribution to the organization. A leader should seek to be a purveyor of fine art, seeing any source of creativity, intelligence, and risk-taking as a valued contribution to the company's prized art collection.

*The goal of a leader should be to coax individuals out of their comfort zone, to expand and grow their personal talents, and to **creatively** apply themselves toward accomplishing their objectives.*

While team members may have different comfort levels with risk, *every* team member should be required to think and act independently and creatively in order to continue his or her personal growth and organizational impact.

The most important aspect of creating a "corporate art collection" is to empower the people who create with a sense of autonomy and fearlessness. To create effectively, the people of the organization need to be focused on envisioning the final result, and not feel bogged down with imagined interpretations or potential pitfalls. We are in the habit of paralyzing much of the greatness within our companies today by focusing on the interpretations from upper management, the acceptance from our peers, and the potential failures we may encounter on the road to creating our accomplishments.

Embracing our creativity is essential for the future success of the U.S. job market, where many of the repetitive jobs have been exported to countries with lower-cost resources. Our biggest potential for growth is in our innovation, which is the primary by-product of our personal creativity.

How does a leader inspire creativity?

Creativity needs to be inspired and cultivated within the organization on a daily basis. Once the team is comfortable in applying their creative juices to a variety of tasks, it will quickly propagate throughout the culture and methods used within the organization. There are many ways to be creative, with endless possibilities and methods for leaders to tap into. Some ideas to get the juices flowing include:

1. **Throw spaghetti at the wall**. Provide an example or encourage teams to make a "straw man" draft to initiate the creative process. It is far easier to create a concept from something that is partially present. Having a draft helps reviewers create an initial image in their mind and calls forth an intuitive response to start the creative process. It encourages them to mold other ideas, feelings, and thoughts around this draft image, until it becomes something that they feel they have personalized and are comfortable with. Nothing can hinder the creative process more than the intimidation of not knowing where to start or what is expected. While care should be taken not to force or limit the creative process by giving an example, it can be a useful tactic if the team is struggling to come up with the initial idea.

2. **There are no "wrong" answers**. Listen and seek to understand all ideas. Capture them all, then help the group to evaluate the list. It is amazing how many ideas are reconsidered after an initial rejection after going through the brainstorming process. Ideas are contagious and

encourage people to continue to explore new territories and perspectives that they may not have thought of initially. It is also important to realize that there are many differing perspectives as to what is "good art." Try to not discount someone's ideas. Capture everything, use it to build upon the creative effort, and discourage judgments.

3. **Learn the art of "facilitation."** Recognize *when* you need to direct, instruct, and facilitate. Facilitation is a two-way street. Try not to "direct" a brainstorming session and recognize that the leader does not always have to be the facilitator. Switch the facilitator role in the group to give people different experiences and a fresh approach to the group dynamics. It can also be very useful to give the entire team formal training on facilitation. This training will help them see the leader's perspective, and can help them to increase their skills for participating or leading group workshops.

4. **Recognize and reward creativity.** Be on the lookout for new ways to do things and for people who have taken initiative to do things differently and take pride in adding their "uniqueness" to the job. People feel proud when their work is appreciated and admired. Build your own team's method of recognition for creative contributions. Good creativity requires strong confidence from all contributors. Recognizing them helps to continually reinforce their confidence and value to the team.

5. **Allow time and freedom for inspiration to occur.** Nothing is worse than trying to force ideas to come to the table if none are present. A leader needs to develop the intuition to know when to drive the process and when to hold back. Sometimes it is helpful to let the team mull over ideas and concepts in their free time, or to let the ideas sink in for a few days to elicit thoughtful responses. If you start early in the task and don't procrastinate, you can keep yourself

and your team from being pressured with deadlines and commitments.

6. **Create diverse teams.** Teams work better with employees who have different backgrounds, skills, and personal styles. Creativity thrives on different viewpoints and interpretations. Make sure to create the environment that allows each diverse personality to come alive and prosper. One way to evaluate if your team has a good mix is to consider how many different viewpoints or ideas are expressed in one of your team's meetings. If the ideas tend to be similar or everyone is not fully engaged, you may want to consider involving people from other departments to help generate new ideas and feedback. Sometimes it just takes one outspoken person or newcomer to breathe fresh air into the team and let others feel comfortable in expressing themselves.

7. **Do different things.** Change settings, meeting styles, topics, and venues to encourage new thoughts or perspectives and eliminate automatic reactions or preset expectations. When we think differently, we act differently, inspiring real change to take place. Remember to not feel pressured as the leader to come up with all the great ideas. Often the best ideas often come from team members who have brought their personal experiences or previous team success stories to the group.

8. **Maintain a *continuous improvement* environment.** If you keep an "evergreen" approach to your team's ideas, processes, and products, it will ensure that things don't get stagnant or predictable. If you fail to maintain an ever-improving environment, you can be sure that your competitive edge and customer's needs are being left behind. Keep change coming, challenge the status quo, and always be revising, revisiting, and re-energizing your products, processes, and people skills.

What does a creative team look like? They are energetic and passionate about what they are delivering. They are secure in their *own* abilities but also understand and appreciate the talents of *others*. They know how to integrate their personal strengths with the strengths of other team members to maximize the team result. A creative team has no concept of preconceived boundaries and does not need encouragement to "think outside the box." If the status quo is acceptable for a company, the employees are encouraged to be complacent and agreeable and rarely look at "sticking their neck out" or stretching for something different or better. If creativity is embraced and encouraged from individuals, teams, and departments, the company will produce enthusiastic employees with inspired results. A creative team feels as much as they think, and knows that creation is an ongoing process that may require some failures to reach their success. However, they realize that these failures can bring the team closer and unify them in their quest to deliver their ultimate, "grand finale."

A balanced leader values creativity and recognizes the benefits that creativity can bring to the organization. She encourages creativity with her employees and in her work environment, as she knows of its ability to strengthen individual contribution, job satisfaction, and overall contribution to the organization.

Inspire Creativity—Personal Exercise

1. What creative things did you do last week?

2. Write ten things you can do differently tomorrow to encourage new thoughts and actions. These can be small, such as "drive a different way to work," or large such as "take up a new hobby."

3. What are three product, process, or people skills that you could challenge to make yourself, your team, or your organization better?

Inspire Creativity—Team Exercise

1. Choose a facilitator within your team and have him or her run a brainstorming exercise in your next team meeting. Teach them the importance of accepting all ideas, challenging and growing new ideas, and passionate engagement.

2. Talk about the "Art of Facilitation" and examine the qualities that are required for this with the team. Review Web sites to look for facilitation tools, tips, or guidance that you can offer your team.

Foster Growth

❝ An inspirational leader sees all situations, the
positive and the negative, as growth opportunities;
unleashing our personal talents, perfecting our
skills, and allowing us to take flight **❞**

Foster Growth

$\mathcal{M}$y proudest leadership experiences have included the times when I have helped individuals advance in their personal growth and careers—each promotion proof of their progress, each success testimony of their confidence, and each win evidence of our camaraderie. An effective leader learns how to make everything a growth experience—reinforcing and rewarding through the positive, while supporting and coaching through the negative. Through both the positive and negative growth opportunities, it is critical for the leader to take a balanced approach, relying on both the masculine and feminine traits to maximize the benefits of the learning experience and heighten the individual's receptivity to the feedback. This balanced approach requires the leader to master both the hard and soft elements of communication, requiring her to be direct and firm in her feedback, yet compassionate and flexible in her style. If she harnesses both the hard and soft elements correctly, and uses her intuition to properly sense the needs of the individual, she can turn any experience into a positive growth opportunity and an occasion for improved loyalty. The balanced leader sees a growth opportunity as not only a chance to improve an individual's personal development, but also as a chance to further an individual's respect and satisfaction with the organization as a whole. She sees the organization as an organic entity, whose health is determined from the collective well-being of those within its walls; expanding and growing from each individual learning experience.

If we focus on the need to *Foster Growth* within the individual, the team, and the company, we will learn to see almost every situation as a potential growth opportunity. A difficult problem, a troubled employee, or an outraged customer can transform into a growth opportunity for everyone involved in both the problem and the solution. These opportunities have the potential to deliver positive impacts, including improved employee confidence, greater customer loyalty, increased knowledge, and insightful lessons for the future. Conversely, if a growth opportunity is handled badly, brushed aside, or neglected, it can lead to negative impacts, including lost business, ambivalent or enraged employees, and mistrust in the organization. Thus, the leader has two choices: 1) To address and turn the negative situation into a growth opportunity, or 2) to ignore or condemn the negative situation and make it an unconstructive experience for all. A leader's actions will make her choice evident in every situation; she cannot avoid making this choice when handling a negative situation in her job. A balanced leader sees the benefits and repercussions from the results of her actions and will always strive to look for ways to **Foster Growth** rather than to condemn or place blame. This is an *active* choice; one that must be proactively made and continuously monitored by the leader to ensure the consistency and candor of her actions.

A leader cannot effectively grow her team if she is addressing growth once a year in a performance review, or as part of a one-time workshop or training event. Because we tend to *see* what we are looking for, it is vital for leaders to actively define clear growth expectations and to aggressively look for opportunities to unlock the potential within others. When a leader focuses on the growth of each individual, she can maximize the contribution each person makes to the team; likewise, when a leader focuses on the growth and expansion of the group, she can maximize the contribution of the collective team. Individual and team growth are not mutually exclusive, as many situations provide growth opportunities for both the individual and the team simultaneously. We've all seen a great difficulty overcome by an individual lift the spirits and the enthusiasm of the team and motivate the collective group to reach higher achievements. All individual and team growth should be fostered continuously, as part of the ongoing leadership challenge. Fostering growth is a dynamic skill, and while the leader should not be expected to be the sole provider of feedback, the leader *is* expected to provide the encouragement and expectations for growth to occur as *part* of the team's experiences, not as something separate and distinct that occurs outside of their daily activities.

The balanced leader can foster growth in her team through the following actions:

1. Create an *Environment* for Growth
2. Provide a Variety of *Perspectives*
3. Pay Attention to the Message *Received*

Create an *Environment* for Growth

It is important for the leader to exhibit the mindset and actions that encourage and elicit personal growth from all team members. A growth-oriented environment is positive, yet realistic about the concept of "perfection" and strives to manage expectations appropriately. It gives us hope that while none of us is perfect, all of us can improve. In order for the leader to get acceptance from her team, she must be realistic and take the approach that improving is an ongoing process for all of us, not a destination that we can magically arrive at one day. Growing requires us to continually look for and experience opportunities which sharpen our current skills, confront our known weaknesses, and give us exposure to new topics and situations. People must be comfortable and trusting in order to feel secure enough to expose themselves to growth opportunities. As we all have experienced as some point in our lives, growth opportunities are not always pretty. What makes a situation a "growth opportunity" is that we are given the *option of failure*. The growth opportunity assumes that *we need to learn* and gives us a *"get out of jail free"* card that we may not have to use, but can call upon if we get into trouble. This growth opportunity/potential failure scenario creates a challenge for the leader who is both trying to support an individual's growth yet needing to successfully complete her objectives. Too often, we are encouraging and supportive of growth, yet hesitant to let our people use their "get out of jail free" card. It is critical to accept that we have to allow for failures in the growth process. A balanced leader accepts this, and leverages her use of growth effectively so she doesn't put her entire team's performance at risk. She creates safe areas within the business—with *allowed buffer zones*—to give team members the room to experiment. She also defines critical areas within the business—ones that may have little to no buffer zones—that require careful watch by experienced team members. She uses her knowledge of the individual needs and her knowledge of the business needs to create growth opportunities *and* reliable outcomes.

The balanced leader can create an environment to *Foster Growth* by:

- **Believing that we all need to grow.** Growth is a requirement for each of us to maintain our satisfaction level within our given role and to further develop our skills, experience, and career.

- **Understanding the growth areas for each individual**. A leader can impact growth more rapidly if she gets to know her people, understands their skills, and uncovers their dreams, to properly address the gaps that need to be filled.

- **Continually stretching oneself.** A leader can serve as a good role model to the team if she actively challenges her own limits and expands her personal growth by naturally operating "outside her comfort zone."

- **Encouraging and rewarding growth.** A leader can make the growth of her people widely known and acknowledged by recognizing individuals when they have gone outside their comfort zone, and rewarding their *efforts*, rather than only celebrating the results.

Provide a Variety of *Perspectives*

The balanced leader needs to first examine growth from the individual's perspective. She must accurately determine the direction the person wants to pursue and the skills or needs the individual requires to reach his or her ultimate destination. The leader must be careful to not limit or assume another's growth needs based on her *perceived* impressions or ideas of what is best for another. To protect against her own impressions, she looks for a variety of growth opportunities and teachers to help support an individual's progression. She understands that she only has so much to teach, and that individuals will maximize their growth potential by increasing their exposure to a variety of people and situations.

We have to separate the ego from leadership. Just because a leader has been chosen doesn't mean that she is the most knowledgeable or experienced person in all subjects. An ego-based leader is one who leads from fear: fear of being wrong, fear of making a mistake, fear of being found out. A balanced leader is one who leads from strength; she understands that the more her people shine and succeed, the more her success will naturally follow. A leader is not responsible for "knowing it all"; she is responsible for helping others and providing them guidance in how to best do their job and grow as individuals. It is important for a leader to provide her team members with a variety of learning experiences and teachers for two reasons: 1) It increases the exposure and growth opportunities for the individual, and 2) it evens out and validates the leader's assessment of the individual. While a leader should always try to be as objective as possible, we all come equipped with our own "colored glasses," our personal perspective that we see through. Because of this inherent "bias," the leader will provide better guidance and make more accurate assessments if she incorporates different perspectives from others involved with the individual.

She gains other perspectives by:

- *Encouraging* people to work with their peers or people outside of their team on special projects or assignments
- *Assigning* a task in a new field or area they have not worked on before
- *Asking* for feedback from others regularly and at different levels in the organization, including peers and other managers

When a leader actively asks for feedback, it helps her understand the bigger picture, bringing balance to her opinions and assessments. The balanced leader listens attentively; she does not interrupt or defend, as she understands that it is critical to her team's growth to learn from each person and each situation. She doesn't take any one view as "fact," but works to assemble the most accurate picture from all of the input provided.

The balanced leader understands the value of perceptions, along with the dangers and realities that they bring. If we realize the inherent power of our own and others' perceptions, we can actively tap into this insight to help in our individual development and to help guide our interactions and relationships with others. How we are being perceived is an important lesson for how we should go forth in our actions. A balanced leader will try to create the most accurate "perception" picture in order to have an unbiased, insightful mechanism for encouragement and personal development.

Pay Attention to the Message *Received*

You would not hook up a fire hose to deliver water to your garden, so make sure to gauge your delivery when providing feedback. *How* you say it is as important as *what* you say. Often our biggest growth opportunities are in the areas where we have the most hesitation due to the difficulty and discomfort of the confrontation required. Having several perspectives can help to provide examples and justification for delivering a tough message, but does not negate the importance of how the message is *received*.

It is important for the balanced leader to deliver both the positive and negative feedback to properly inspire and develop her team members. Delivering positive feedback is often done immediately and is typically done without much planning or introspection due to the ease of its delivery. Negative feedback, however, is often neglected or mismanaged due to the sensitivity and time required to ensure it is properly delivered and received. All feedback needs to be fair and constructive. Just as you don't want to gold-plate or go overboard on the positive, you can't be too pessimistic or demanding on the negative. A leader must develop a relationship that is based on fairness and trust, and can draw from these qualities when delivering both the good and bad feedback. If a leader is too positive, other team members may feel that the person has been "singled out" and has an unfair advantage in the team. If a leader is too negative, the team will seek to defend *"one of their own"* and rebel against the leader, or worse, they may distance themselves from that individual or the problem. The balanced leader carefully approaches the delivery of her message to maximize the growth benefit from the experience. She is careful not to internalize, exaggerate, or deflect the issue on others. She takes the ownership and the responsibility of delivering the message, and keeps her objectivity to ensure that the growth issues of the other person do not impact her internal confidence and emotional stability. It is critical for the leader to understand the focus of the feedback; the focus *should not* be on what's best or easiest for the person delivering the message, the focus *should* be on doing the right thing to support the ongoing performance and development of the person receiving the message.

In planning the delivery of feedback, a leader should ask the following questions:

- What are the facts and the overall perception of the experience?
- What is the impact to the person and/or the team?
- Is there a consequence if the person does not change or learn from this feedback?
- What is the potential for success if they change and can learn from this?

By focusing the discussion on the perceptions of others, the growth potential available, and the support that you and others can provide, the receiver is more likely to see the constructive feedback as a "growth experience" rather than a negative attack. Most importantly, the leader must monitor the response and the progress after the constructive feedback to positively reinforce the changes made, or to look for other ways to reinforce the change if it is not being readily adopted. These feedback sessions should be looked at as a standard component within the leader's daily leadership style, rather than isolated occurrences that can be ignored or dismissed. If the leader takes this daily "coaching" approach, she can make growing a casual experience, one that is comfortable, respectful, and appreciated, and most importantly, one that inspires introspection and behavioral change in the individual.

The balanced leader strives to combine the hard and soft elements of *Fostering Growth* to maximize the potential of her team. She works to create a trusting environment, a fair and objective perspective, and consistent feedback as part of her ongoing leadership style. Through this process, she is able to ensure that she provides the right opportunities and constructive guidance to make the most of individual performance, job satisfaction, and career potential throughout the organization.

Foster Growth—Personal Exercise

1. Visualize and list your strengths and weaknesses.

2. Pick one of your predominant weaknesses; think about how this weakness manifests in various situations in your life: your job, family life, and personal activities.

3. Visualize sitting down with an imaginary "boss" who wants to help you improve this weakness.

4. What skills or emotions do you need to master to overcome this weakness?

5. What situations bring out this weakness? What skills or practices can you develop to manage yourself in these situations?

6. What opportunities do you need to be exposed to in order to learn how to master this weakness in your life?

7. Imagine that this imaginary "boss" is putting together a plan to give you everything you need to overcome this weakness. What does that plan look like?

Foster Growth—Team Exercise

1. In your next team meeting or in one-on-one sessions with your employees, ask if they have enough growth opportunities in their daily job. Talk with them about where they would like to go, what they enjoy doing, and their satisfaction level with the team.

2. Ask if they are interested in devoting some time to mentor or encourage growth in others.

3. Make a commitment for each of you to look for growth opportunities over the next month and report back on what you have each found that is in alignment with their desired growth path.

4. Make a point of ensuring that each team member always has at least one growth opportunity special project or assignment throughout the year; monitor and ask them to report to the group on this task to encourage the growth focus and expectations within the team.

5. Reward the additional time or efforts spent by others to enhance their growth; use these growth experiences to create more opportunities or career moves in your team.

Cultivate Culture

" An engaging leader inspires joy and
creativity in others; she is attentive
to her team's interactions and *actively*
pursues a positive culture "

Cultivate Culture

I've been through so many changes within every company I've ever worked for that it is hard to accurately describe what the "culture" was within each company. I remain optimistic that more corporations will see value in developing a well-defined, practiced culture that is positive, embracing, and consistent across all departments and people. I can't help but imagine how great a company could be if it had consistently high performers properly executing their job in an environment that encouraged teamwork, innovation, and success. I eagerly anticipate the day when our corporations embrace culture as a critical component of its success, and treat it with the same measurement and respect as its revenue and operating earnings.

Our business and leadership environments are in a perpetual state of change. Every day there are new accounts of corporate mergers, acquisitions, divestitures, restructurings, and workforce reductions. With each change come countless taskforces and discussions concerning revenue growth, cost savings, and enhanced service offerings. Unfortunately, while undergoing these major changes, there seems to be a predominant lack of focus on the impact *to the people* in the organization or avoidance of the *real issues* facing the organization. Our perpetual state of change has encouraged a culture of distraction and avoidance, one that keeps us from often getting to the root cause of the problems facing the organization. Often it is not until after the fact—after the "decreased morale," "high turnover," or "loss of business" that companies realize they need to take the culture of the organization seriously.

Cultures are characterized by the following principles:

1. Cultures Are Created *by the People*

2. A Culture Is *Always* Present

Cultures Are Created *by the People*

Corporate culture represents a collective attitude about an organization formed out of the opinions, feelings, words, and actions of its people. A culture cannot be forced *on* people; it evolves over time, as a result of the leadership and policies they embrace. Until this is recognized, organizations will continue to force corporate objectives, mission statements, and ethical standards as they work zealously to define a *culture*. Ironically, the more they force the "friendliness" of the new culture, the more cynicism and defiance seems to predominate. You cannot effectively force a culture or assume the culture by talking to a select few; nor can you presume that the culture is a natural by-product of events or results. Revenues can be up, turnover down, and the culture can still be a mess. Culture must be carefully cultivated, with a strong focus on employee involvement and realistic assessment, to create an environment that maximizes results, inspires trust, and provides a unique "personality" that employees and business partners *want* to be associated with.

A Culture Is *Always* Present

This is both good news and bad news. The good news is that a leader can confidently work towards defining the ever-present culture and integrating it throughout her organization. The bad news is that *a leader who ignores the culture will get one anyway*. It is impossible for two or more people to be together without an inherent culture being formed between them. If the thoughts, words, and actions of the people are encouraging and considerate, a positive culture will emerge. If they are pessimistic and skeptical, a negative culture will be created. If they are disinterested and impartial, an ambivalent culture will be created. No matter what great facts the people present or the results they produce, the culture they have created will impact everyone positively or negatively. Understanding this gives the leader reason for actively cultivating the culture, so she is in control over the type of company she builds, rather than being at the mercy of an undefined culture created without her stewardship.

The balanced leader understands that culture is not created from a corporate document, a one-time event, or a town meeting. She realizes that creating a true company culture is intentional and must be supported consistently by all leaders throughout the organization on a daily basis. To be effective, a culture has to be narrowly defined so it can be clearly understood by everyone, while expansive enough to be "experienced" by everyone across the organization. It must transcend departments, positions, and personal backgrounds. The balanced leader seeks to define a culture using the masculine and feminine traits to create an environment that is clear and decisive, while also relying on the communication and compassion requirements that allow it to be effectively embraced. A culture cannot be stagnant, and has to keep up with the dynamic nature of the company. The balanced leader makes *culture* a verb, encouraging a culture that is both realistic and dynamic as she works to define it and monitor it *with* the people of the company. She knows that it requires active engagement and practice in order to be fully realized throughout the organization. If it is not an active practice, and looked at as a passive by-product, it will be destined to remain as a corporate "concept," identified only by the dusty wall-hanging in the lobby.

Too many leaders associate the *morale* of the people with the *culture* of the organization. This is similar to someone focusing on starvation when trying to evalute the overall nutritional needs of the planet. While morale is a natural by-product of a company's culture, the culture provides a much bigger opportunity to proactively define and create what is wanted, as opposed to avoiding one element that is not wanted. Too often, morale is only considered when there is a problem, after the effects of a neglected culture become apparent, when leaders rush off armed with posters, taglines, and town hall meetings to fix the "morale" problem. Ironically, the numerous attempts at fixing "morale" tend to *add* to the cynicism and mistrust of those impacted; invoking the *"here we go again"* experience.

*The balanced leader understands the need to have the organization actively face culture as **part** of the change; rather than assuming its outcome **after** the change.*

Culture is designed from the onset as being a long-term approach to employee and customer satisfaction. It is meant to encompass the "hard" elements of vision statements, corporate objectives, and facilities, as well as the "softer" elements of loyalty, employee/customer satisfaction, and personal interactions. It is meant to be all-inclusive and designed for everyone in the company: executives, management, employees, customers, partners, and vendors. Unlike morale, which may vary from different sites or groups within a company, culture should be broad enough to be applied and measured consistently across all teams and divisions across the entire organization.

When a positive culture is established, the internal loyalty and satisfaction of the group is increased by the following:

- **More Clarity in Direction**. If people are taught the vision, targets, and expectations or an organization, and see it executed on a daily basis, they are better able to internalize the statement and apply it to their daily tasks.

- **Greater Loyalty.** If people understand the vision of the team and see that it motivates positive actions and personal responsibility across the group, they are more likely to want to be involved with the group and support the decisions of others in the group.

- **More Engagement.** If people understand the "rules" of how the organization works, including its eagerness to tap into its people, they are more likely to participate and tend to be more passionate when they engage.

- **Improved Performance.** If people understand the objectives, trust their leaders and their organization, and engage with enthusiasm and passion, better results will be obtained as a whole. Having a common culture can be a strong method to unify various departments, business units, and teams across an organization to effectively impact bottom-line results.

The balanced leader uses the following tactics to *Cultivate Culture*:

1. **Communicate a clear definition.** Until management clearly defines who and what the company is, they will not be able to consistently set or work toward the goals of the organization. Leaders must see the development of the mission statement, vision, and objectives for the organization as a first step in defining the culture, not as the final endpoint. It is critical that once defined, it must be consistently understood and embraced across the organization to have meaning.

2. **Show concern for the work environment.** The leader should draw attention to the needs of the people, their issues, concerns, and general satisfaction with the company. She can further empower them to provide suggestions and work toward having all employees take ownership for their contributions to the culture.

3. **Define a road map of acceptable and unacceptable behavior.** In a time of change, there will be many moving parts, with employees and customers unsure of how they will be impacted personally and professionally. A road map that is openly communicated and reinforced during the change can help increase buy-in for the change and reduce any uncertainty or suspicion in the group. The leader's secret weapon is to provide enough convincing evidence and positive examples to make it *easier* to buy in than to doubt. Her work is to strengthen the confidence for those already on board and make it harder to be one of the naysayers.

4. **Make it relevant to all.** In order to make the culture pervasive, the leader must consider all internal and external contributors when developing her culture road map. She must understand the critical importance of how customers, suppliers, contractors, and other corporate divisions will perceive changes and ensure her message is broad enough to be applicable and understood by all, yet specific enough to form a *personality* across the organization. She values those external to her company, such as partners and customers, and includes them in communications and assessments to ensure their satisfaction along the way.

5. **Consistently reinforce the message.** The leader must look at the culture as a living, breathing element of the organization. Once defined and clearly communicated across the company, it must be continually reinforced through the marketing, internal/external communication, and the daily interactions within the people working *for* and *with* the company. The balanced leader looks to the surveys and feedback as the "hard" monitoring, as well as the "softer," more subjective elements such as cafeteria and water-cooler discussions, personal attitudes, and one-on-one

interactions. She takes responsibility to engage others to build the culture, and doesn't sit back and "hope" it catches on.

The balanced leader recognizes there are formal and informal ways to build culture within the team. The formal methods are proactive, sanctioned communications provided to everyone in a highly visible format, while the less formal are one-on-one discussions, daily actions, or personal chitchat that are communicated on an individual basis, with limited or no visibility.

Formal and Informal Methods for Building Culture:

Formal Methods	Informal Methods
Defined vision and objectives	Daily interactions and decisions by executives
Corporate-sponsored communications	One-on-one manager/ employee discussions
Internal or external marketing	Lunch or personal interactions
Customer communications	Comments/actions in meetings
Corporate and team-sponsored events	Activities/results highlighted by the leader
Job expectations and objectives	Activities done by the leader
Rules of engagement	Customer/external interactions

A leader should understand the importance of both formal and informal methods to establish an effective culture within her team. If a leader reinforces just the formal, then efforts can be perceived as hypocritical or unrealistic for the day-to-day environment. If a leader reinforces just the informal, then corporate support may not be adequately communicated, which can lead to misunderstandings in how the culture is interpreted and applied across the entire organization. Devoted leaders must seize all opportunities to build upon the culture they envision, using both the formal and informal methods.

While a big change offers the opportunity to emphasize "new" or "changed" culture, leaders *do not need to wait for a big change* to focus on establishing a strong, positive culture. A leader should look for *any* opportunity to highlight the importance of the attitudes and actions of individuals impacting the culture. For instance, a project team may have a leader who realizes the importance of the culture within the team, and proactively builds and defines the culture for that team. A task force can work to take responsibility for the culture of their group, and a manager can work to cultivate the culture with her direct reports. Culture is *everyone's* responsibility.

The unfortunate reality is that few people can say that they have been associated with a company that has a positive, well-defined, consistent culture. Perhaps it is a result of the constant change of people and direction that prevents a healthy culture from emerging. However, it will be critical for successful companies of the future to learn how to effectively *sustain* a consistent culture while embracing the need for change to remain competitive. The balanced leader appreciates the momentum generated by a positive culture, and realizes its benefits to the "bottom line," customer satisfaction, and employee retention.

Emphasize Culture—Personal Exercise

1. Think about *your* definition of a "positive culture"; envision your team having an environment that encourages everyone to be actively engaged, to operate at peak performance, and to have a satisfying and rewarding work experience.

2. Think about the attributes that you consider as part of this "positive culture."

3. For each attribute, define the actions that are required to encourage this behavior throughout a team or company.

4. What do you need to make these attributes a reality? Brainstorm ways that *you* could encourage these actions on a day-to-day basis and what support you would need from your senior management.

5. Make a list of the actions you could start doing now to help encourage this positive culture with your team.

6. Think about how you could bring forward your list of items required from senior management to your leadership team.

Cultivate Culture—Team Exercise

1. In your next team meeting, ask your team what they think the current culture is within your team and company.

2. Ask them what attributes they feel are part of a positive culture.

3. Brainstorm ways that you can all start acting to influence changes in the current culture they are experiencing.

4. Commit to having regular updates or feedback from the team on the changes recommended.

5. Look for ways to let senior management know the feedback from the team regarding the current culture and show evidence of the positive changes going on from the proactive approach within the team.

Lead from the Heart

❝ An intuitive leader equally values her internal
guidance and her external connectivity;
she inspires others to be personally engaged
and passionate in their efforts **❞**

Lead from the Heart

*A*ny manager can recite objectives or provide instruction; an effective leader has a strong *passion* for what she is communicating, and makes others *feel* it, rather than simply *hear* it. Good leaders need to excite, energize, and make others believe in *the images and beliefs they carry in both their mind and heart*. I've had the good fortune of having passionate, engaging leaders who inspired and motivated our teams to achieve great success. I've also had a few cases of the ego-charged, personality challenged leaders who failed to elicit any engagement or support from the teams they led. I've never seen a passionate leader who didn't show his or her personal, emotional side to the organization. A good leader must draw upon their mind and heart to fully engage the people and to effectively make a *connection*. This connection is fundamental to the leader's ability to inspire and motivate the team to accomplish their goals. While it is necessary to have the business acumen—the knowledge, experience, and supervisory skill to manage others, it is essential to actively demonstrate *heart* to provide the passion, enthusiasm, and engagement to effectively lead.

Leading from the Heart appeals to the emotional side of people and provides a common ground that we can all identify and connect with. A leader who leads from the heart uses this passion to drive all of her goals and communications with her team. This emotional leader doesn't save her heartfelt words or actions for the occasional sympathetic action or passionate speech, but instead uses them in her daily interactions. She *feels* everything just as she *thinks* everything. Through her consistent emotional appeal to her team, she not only reveals her own beliefs, but also communicates the strong need for her team members to passionately engage. She opens herself up to show others that they need to open up as well, in order to fully believe in the goal they will all reach together. This emotional connection is something that can appeal to all people in the organization, regardless of titles, positions, geographies, or experience. We've all seen the fact-based CEO make company-wide speeches that sound great to investors or in the boardroom, but go flat when presented to the hundreds or thousands of workers focused on their day-to-day jobs in locations far from the corporate office. Using a heart-based approach to appeal to the passions and needs of the people can turn this flat, tedious speech into a compelling call to action. *Leading from the Heart* isn't an option or something that can be attributed to a personal leadership style; *it is a requirement that must be used in order to effectively engage the people of an organization.* Leading with the *mind* may get tasks completed, but **Leading from the Heart** will get fully engaged, motivated team members to accomplish amazing things.

Leading from the Heart requires both strong will and emotional passion. It requires the leader to believe strongly in *what* she is doing and care deeply for *who* she impacts. We have all seen leaders who have a strong will and can lead by objectives, but do not properly acknowledge the importance of the people; making them moderately effective at completing tasks, but less effective with motivating and engaging their team. Some leaders genuinely care about their people, but fail to have a clear direction or objectives to guide them, allowing them to emotionally connect with their team, but seldom reaching peak performance. And many times, we see the leader who brings strong intelligence and work experience to a job, but lacks the people skills and time commitments to effectively manage others, forcing them to get sucked into the habit of doing more than leading. While it may be an impossible quest to find the "perfect" leader, a leader can learn to be effective through combining the fundamental business skills of facts, objectives, and metrics with the heartfelt emotional skills of passion, intuition, and encouragement. A leader's job is to find balance—in herself, in her team, and across the organization.

Leading from the Heart requires equal parts *internal conviction* and *external connectivity*. The leader needs to be strong in her beliefs and objectives in order to be sincere when she is convincing her team to follow her direction. It is essential for the leader to have a firm grasp on her internal beliefs and be passionate and diligent in her approach to achieving her goals. If she doesn't feel passion about *what* she is doing, it will not matter if she can effectively communicate, as she won't have anything inspiring to say. In order to effectively motivate action and inspire loyalty, a leader needs to be a *master of both the content and the delivery.*

An effective leader understands that all people are different, and realizes the need for using intuition and communication skills to navigate between the different gradients of strength and compassion, in order to best relate to each individual need. Because she relies on her internal guidance system to adjust her styles, she can easily switch from a formal presentation to an informal discussion or from a casual conversation to an organized meeting. The leader can quickly interpret, adjust, and develop her approach to best fit the situation at hand. This "instant customization" requires her to trust in her "gut feelings," do her homework ahead of time, and have her faithful set of tools with her at all times—her intelligence, wit, and common sense. The balanced leader has learned the art of connecting with other people, allowing her to make chameleon-like changes based on her surroundings, without sacrificing her internal beliefs and convictions. She has mastered the ability to be tough yet easygoing, firm yet flexible, driven yet tolerant, to get her point across while appealing to a fair outcome.

Leading from the Heart requires the leader to have the following characteristics:

- A *desire to reach a fair outcome* for all people and opinions in a situation.

- A *continuous improvement philosophy* that drives introspection and inspiration to make things better for the organization.

- The ability to *accept the humanity* of herself and others by realizing the imperfections, learning experiences, and growth that are a natural part of life's wins and losses.

- An *inclusive approach* to make tolerance the rule while eliminating biases within herself and the group.

- A *willingness to open up to others* and to connect on a personal, professional level.

- The ability to *trust in "gut feelings"* to effectively interpret and probe to get to the truth.

- The *diligence* to keep moving in the desired direction, to communicate, and to modify the actions of her team to reach the collective goal.

The effective leader understands that people will connect with her message if they are given an appropriate amount of time to adapt and contribute to it, as opposed to a direction that is *forced suddenly* on them. It is more believable and practical for people in the organization to internalize a leader's messages if the leader continuously builds upon a consistent vision and provides practical examples. Taking small steps to inspiring others also allows for more flexibility and readjustment from the leader as they move forward. It allows her to "tune in" the messages and guidance signals from her *heart*. This slow and consistent method is also more forgiving, as it is not as dependent on a single event, or one compelling speech; but rather depends more on the day-to-day contact and the consistency of *words and actions* across the evolving organization.

To put the concepts of Leading from the Heart into practice, the leader can apply the following actions:

- **Separate the Ego from the "Common Good".** The heartfelt leader will embrace the ability to change direction, admit mistakes, or rethink ideas as she gauges the impacts of her decisions. She is committed to remaining "objective" in how she views the organization and its potential. She reminds herself that this isn't about her; it's about the success of the business and fulfillment of the team.

- **Rely on Intuition.** As a leader is gathering data and making conclusions, she needs to remain committed to focus on her perceptions and her emotional guidance to lead her decision-making. She will maximize the benefit and impact of her results by combining both the *facts* and the *feelings* in the organization.

- **Continually Monitor the Pulse.** The effective leader realizes that she needs consistent, frequent data points when she is making decisions for her organization. Her goal is to secure the health of the organization at all times. She realizes that the organization is a dynamic ecosystem that must be monitored regularly, and sets out to establish a culture that is self-correcting by encouraging her team to take ownership of critical metrics and adopting mechanisms to allow for adjustments.

- **Maintain a Consistent Rhythm.** The intuitive leader understands the need for a consistent, regular heartbeat within the organization. While she may enjoy the occasional adrenaline rush associated with a big win or team success, she does not sacrifice the comfortable cadence that the team returns to easily as the business ebbs and flows. She is sensitive to the daily rhythms of her team and interjects or reduces stress in the environment as needed to maintain a steady pulse.

- **Have an Open Mind.** The emotional leader recognizes that individuals need to contribute in order to be fully engaged and passionate in the outcome. She strives to encourage fresh ideas and individual approaches and tries to not get too comfortable with anything for too long. She introduces new stimuli to spawn ideas, asks for input, and is willing to change with the people and needs of the organization.

- **Focus on the Process.** The effective leader remains dedicated to the people and processes in the organization and trusts that customer satisfaction and shareholder value will naturally follow. The leader works from inside the team outward and keeps her attention fixed on the factors that she can control. By monitoring and focusing on the process, she can make adjustments along the way and *feel secure on a daily basis* that her team will reach the final outcome, rather than setting a desired outcome and hoping or assuming that it will be reached.

When a leader combines the "nuts and bolts" of management with the intuition and caring of "heart," she can effectively unlock the potential within others and unleash the infinite possibilities within the organization; she can *effectively lead*. The effective leader must not only *recognize* the need for this "mind" and "heart" approach, but she must also be *accountable* in her daily words and actions for putting the approach into practice. It is her obligation as a leader to set the objectives, inspire the passion, and to consistently reinforce the message.

Developing our ability to lead with passion and conviction is an ongoing process, continually being developed through our learning experiences and individual styles. By recognizing and utilizing both our masculine and feminine traits, we can learn to be effective, balanced leaders. This balanced leadership approach can begin to evolve by applying the concepts contained in each of chapter of this book.

*We can effectively **Lead from the Heart** when we learn to: Encourage Authenticity, Create a Family, Assume Authority, Emanate Strength, Practice Kindness, Advertise Value, Inspire Creativity, Foster Growth, and Cultivate Culture.*

Notes

Notes

Acknowledgements

This book has been in my head for many years. It has come about from journals, scratch pads in hotel rooms, and thoughts on airplanes. It has been created with the patience and always-inspiring words of my husband, Eric Fisher, the help from my good friend, Linda Siegel, and my friends and family who have helped encourage and sustain me through the never-ending process of writing my first book. I am also very grateful to Lena Shiffman, the talented artist who brought the principles in this book to life through her beautiful illustrations. I encourage you to visit the website, www.FSLeadership.com to experience the beauty of the full-color inspirational artwork and products.

I hope this book is an inspiration to fellow leaders to create a more balanced leadership approach in the stressful, bottom-line-focused environments prevalent in our corporations today. Writing it has been an amazing growth and learning experience and will undoubtedly help me in my leadership practices moving forward. I hope for its success, but will be satisfied if it sits on my mother and my daughter's bookshelves (as well as my own!).

This book is evidence of the results we can each achieve if we listen closely to the ever-present guidance and intuition we receive from God on a daily basis, and fully engage our minds and hearts to act on this guidance to realize our full potential. May you always be guided by inspiration and persistent in your actions to achieve your dreams!

Printed in the United States
112713LV00004B/229-648/P